Developing Part-Singing Skills
in School-Age Musicians

one accord

by Georgia A. Newlin, DMA

Roger Sams, editor

No part of this publication may be reproduced in any form or by any means, except where indicated as reproducible, without the prior written permission of the publisher.

COVER IMAGE: SHUTTERSTOCK ©ARGUS

Copyright © 2016 by MIE Publications
5228 Mayfield Road • Cleveland, Ohio 44124
(800) 888-7502

www.MusicIsElementary.com

Acknowledgements

"Curiosity has always gotten me into trouble. It has also led to some of the greatest moments of learning in my life."

Thank you to my parents and siblings for endless encouragement – there has always been ample supply of support for musical endeavors in our household.

Thank you to my school and church music teachers for, rather than thwarting my inquisitiveness, encouraging me to work toward becoming a better musician.

Thank you to my exemplary teachers and mentors for sharing their incredible talents and energies: Jane Pippart-Brown, Sallie Ferribee, Sr. Mary Alice Hein, Ed Bolkovac, Rita Klinger, Lenci Igo, Ildikó Herboly Kocsár, Éva Vendrei, Gabi Thész, Erzsébet Hegyi, Laurdella Folkes-Levy, and Anne Laskey.

Thank you to extraordinary colleagues who have pushed me to think with boundless limits so that I have become a much better teacher: Brent Gault, Nyssa Brown, Kathy Kuddes, Susan Glass, Joy Anderson, and members of the Upper Adams Fine Arts Team.

Thank you to Naomi Cohen for working with my undergraduate Music Education majors at Adelphi University as an Artist-in-Residence, and for sharing the beautiful song, *Lo Yisa Goy*, which is used in this text.

Thank you to Eva Floyd for the ideas of cruise control and the counting catch used to demonstrate canonic singing and catch in this text.

Thank you to Bethany Houff for allowing me to use her arrangement of "All the Pretty Little Horses", and for the countless hours of reading through the songs and text for error detection.

Thank you to Dawn Houff for the wonderfully fastidious last minute read-through.

Thank you to Ruth Boshkoff, Patrick Freer, Lynnel Joy Jenkins, and Dan LeJune for their endorsements of this book.

Thank you to Roger Sams at Music Is Elementary for his encouragement and editorial expertise and to Marie Smith for the beautiful layout of this book – both are greatly appreciated.

Finally, to all of my students (K-12, university, Kodály workshops) and choir members who have believed over the years that what I have had to teach has been valuable, this book is for you. It is my hope that you will share the information with the same love and dedication to learners that I have felt for each of you.

With much love, this book is dedicated to Beth, Liza & Sylvie.

Contents

Introduction 6

Part-Singing Sequencing 6

Tools for Teaching Part-Singing Skills 10

Chapter 1   *Teaching Procedures for* **Readiness Skills** 12

Chapter 2   *Teaching Procedures for* **Singing Skills** 15

Chapter 3   *Teaching Procedures for* **Rhythmic Part-work Skills** 33

Chapter 4   *Teaching Procedures for* **Melodic Part-work Skills** 47

Chapter 5   *Teaching Procedures for* **Part-Singing Skills in Polyphony** ... 71

Chapter 6   *Teaching Procedures for* **Part-Singing Skills in Homophony** ... 116

Alphabetical Song List 154

Elementary School Song List 156

Middle School Song List 157

High School Song List 158

Three Note Melodies 159

Do-centered Melodies 159

Blues Scale Melodies 160

La-centered Melodies 161

Modal & Mode-like Melodies 161

Time Signatures 162

Songs with Complete Texts or Additional Versus in Languages
other than English 165

Appendix A - Glossary 166
Appendix B - Resources 169
Appendix C - Solfège Syllables 171
Appendix D - Translation and Adaptation of Non-English Text 172

Index of Topics and Song Titles 179

About the Author: Georgia A. Newlin 182

INTRODUCTION

Part-Singing Sequencing

THIS BOOK IS WRITTEN FOR MUSIC EDUCATORS who wish to experience a higher level of success in leading school-age musicians to sing in multiple parts. This curriculum assists music educators so that by considering every discrete skill of the part-singing process, each with their own teaching sequence, putting them in a proper order, and using high-quality musical materials, their singers can become better choral musicians.

It is important to understand that each music educator needs to consciously point out to young musicians what it is that they are doing – by name and definition – so that it becomes a mindful act of musicianship when they are singing in parts.

The thorough comprehension of same, different, and similar is the absolute basis of part-work. Older singers will (most likely) already understand the concepts of comparatives such as fast/slow, high/low, loud/soft, the beat divided by two/the beat divided by three and same/different/similar in form; however the youngest musicians will need to be consciously taught.

For each part-work skill there are suggested songs for the elementary, middle school, and high school levels but many are interchangeable between multiple levels depending on the situation (such as advanced elementary singers in a select community choir versus beginner singers at the high school level). The teacher must take into account the skills of the singers and, particularly, the appropriateness of the text and meaning of each piece. Easier pieces sung in languages other than English often challenge older singers due to learning the text. This allows the ensemble to work on less complicated part-singing skills but keeps the singers interested because of the language demands.

The songs are laid out in suggested keys but may be transposed to any key that is appropriate to the ensemble's vocal range.

The original purchaser of this book is authorized to reproduce and use the individual songs within the educational setting for which this book is purchased. However, the reproducible songs may not be reprinted or electronically reproduced in whole or in part as a reproducible book or collection, or for use as a handout for an entire school district, teacher work group, in-service meeting, multi-school honors ensemble or any other purpose without the written permission of the publisher.

Teaching/Learning Progression

The ideas of FOUNDATION (preparation through performance), CORE KNOWLEDGE (make conscious of musical understanding), and REHEARSE & ENRICH (developing musicianship skills through practice) are important in good planning so that the singers are not constantly trying to learn a song at the same time they are learning the part-singing skill. One of the most egregious errors made by many music educators is asking singers to learn the song and the skill at the same time. It is important that in most cases the singers must each be able to individually sing the tune very well before adding the part-work skill. This requires prior planning for earlier rehearsals so that the ensemble either sight-reads or learns by rote a new tune in one or two lessons so the tune can be used to teach a part-singing skill in a second or third later lesson. This sequence can occur over concurrent lessons or, with the more difficult tunes (languages, rhythmic intricacy, etc.), can occur over a broader span of lessons.

Concerts & Performancess

All of these songs can be programmed in concerts and can be performed in multiple ways such as using instruments to perform the second part, or by singing the same song with two or three different part-work techniques in succession, or with singers improvising, or by having singers write and perform their own accompaniments.

Likewise, none of these pieces need be programmed but can be used as warm-ups, for sight-reading, and for instruction that leads to using each particular part-work skill in choral octavos and larger works. For older singers who have already performed some of these part-work skills, these techniques can be used to allow singers to learn and use the name of the skill and give them ways to practice with clarity.

Teaching/Learning Timelines

Based on the modules laid out on page 8-9.

Elementary (1 to 2 meetings per week)

- K–1 = Readiness Module
- 1–2 = Singing Module and into Part-Work Module
- 2–5 = Part-Work Module and into beginning of Part-Singing Module

Middle School (3 meetings per week)

- 1st semester = Readiness Module, Singing Module, Part-Work Module
- 2nd semester = beginning to the midpoint of the Part-Singing Module

High School (3 meetings per week)

- 1st semester = Readiness, Singing, and Part-Work Modules, begin Part-Singing Module
- 2nd semester = finish Part-Singing Module

Organization of the Sequence of Part-work/Part-Singing Skills

This sequence is based on research from multiple sources including teachers and researchers in the Kodály, Orff Schulwerk, and choral provinces. Having collected as much available part-singing pedagogical information as possible, it was compiled and categorized systematically by looking for sequential commonalities, resulting in a teaching hierarchy of part-singing skills.

A labeling system was used to identify every step of each part-work and part-singing sequence in each body of literature. After each step was identified [Appendix A, Glossary, page 166], steps that were similar were classified into groups of: readiness, singing, part-work (rhythmic and melodic) and part-singing (polyphony and homophony). From this classification a hierarchy was established from the frequency with which part-singing types appear in numerous sequences from the literature [Appendix B, Resources, page 169]. A range of topics was mentioned, from unison singing (cited the most frequently and ranked first) to diatonic scales (cited the least frequently and ranked last).

From the following two ideas the entire sequence arises:

part-work – the ability to perform and maintain one's own part in music while another part (instrumental, hand signs, body percussion, rhythmic, melodic, vocal, etc.) is being performed simultaneously; part-singing is a type of part-work.

part-singing – the ability to sing and maintain one's own vocal part in music while another vocal part is being performed simultaneously; includes 2-part (bicinia), 3-part (tricinia), 4-part, and multiple-division vocal music.

The sequencing of part-singing begins with readiness and singing skills, moves to part-work skills (being mindful to teach both rhythmic and melodic skills interspersed over the course of time), then heads to part-singing skills when the singers are ready (being sure to include both polyphonic and homophonic music), as this flow-chart demonstrates:

Readiness Module

comparatives
- fast/slow
- high/low
- loud/soft
- beat divided by two/beat divided by three
- same/different/similar

use of the voice for singing and speaking

Singing Module

unison singing
echo song
dialogue song
singing games

Part-Work Module

Rhythmic

beat
- beat while stationary
- beat through locomotor movement
- beat through body ostinato

beat division
- beat verses beat division

rhythm
- beat versus beat division versus rhythm

rhythmic ostinato
multiple rhythmic ostinati
rhythm canon
rhythm body canon

Melodic

antiphonal singing *(groups)*
chain phrases *(individuals)*
call and response
drone/pedal point
melodic ostinato
multiple melodic ostinati

Part-Singing Module

Polyphony

canonic singing
combined canonic singing and ostinato
partner songs
layered song
canon
catch
descant
counter melody
two parts with self (polyphonic)
quodlibet
madrigal
multi-division polyphonic music

Homophony

hand sign singing
interval singing
harmonic ending
round
chord root singing
vocal chording
parallel harmony
two parts with self (homophonic)
glee
chorale/hymn
multi-division homophonic music

Tools for Teaching Part-Singing Skills

If you have not yet selected tools for teaching music literacy, the following are suggested. However, this part-singing sequence can be achieved regardless of the melodic system or rhythmic system used.

Solfège & Hand Signs

By using solfège and hand signs within a movable do/la-based minor solfège system [Appendix C, page 171], many music educators have been better able to help their singers learn musical skills than without these tools. Singers learn to organize sound internally by using solfège and hand signs to help recall how the sounds relate to each other – particularly by feeling the size of an interval in one's voice in relationship to the kinesthetic movement of the hand signs. Giving singers multiple opportunities to become familiar with and use solfège and hand signs allows them to become more fluent musicians.

Rhythm Syllables

By using beat-function rhythm syllables, many music educators have been better able to lead their singers to rhythm precision by helping singers organize sound in time in relation to the beat. Each part of the beat, the beat division, and the subdivision are represented by different syllables. Giving singers multiple opportunities to become familiar with and use beat-function rhythm syllables also allows them to become more fluent musicians.

Examples of beat-function rhythm syllable systems (demonstrating four 16th notes) include:

Galin-Paris-Chevé *(ta-fe-te-fe)*

Music Learning Theory *(du-ta-de-ta)*

Takadimi *(ta-ka-di-mi)*

Bertaux/Foulkes-Levy *(ta-ki-ti-ki)*

Languages other than English

The following languages are included in this volume: French, German, Hebrew, Italian, Latin, Liberian, Provençal, Spanish, Yoruban. Generally speaking, the students can use the internet to research and learn the pronunciations. The following resources are highly recommended:

Translations and Annotations of Choral Repertoire (earthsongs)

- **Vol I:** Sacred Latin Texts
- **Vol II:** German Texts/IPA Pronunciation Guide
- **Vol III:** French and Italian Texts
- **Vol IV:** Hebrew Texts

Pronouncing Guide to French, German, Italian, Spanish (Carl Fischer)

The following languages are transliterated in this volume: Japanese, Polynesian, Russian. The characters of each original language have been changed into corresponding letters and syllables of the English language. Singers can produce (pretty close to) the correct sounds by singing what they see with English pronunciation.

If you prefer not to have students sing in a specific language, they can sing in solfège syllables, on absolute pitch names, or on a neutral syllable. In addition, if you choose not to use a song at all because of the language, choose one of the other songs listed on the page to work on that particular skill.

Translations and adaptations of all non-English texts can be found in Appendix D, page 172.

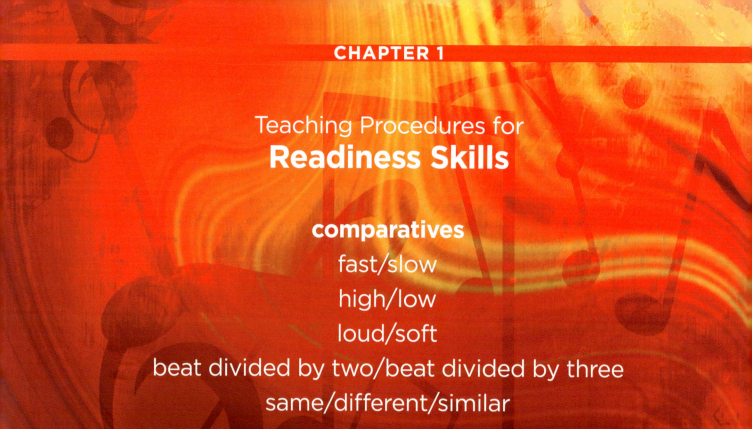

CHAPTER 1

Teaching Procedures for Readiness Skills

comparatives
fast/slow
high/low
loud/soft
beat divided by two/beat divided by three
same/different/similar

use of the voice for singing and speaking

---

comparatives – *comparing and identifying things in music that are the same, different, or similar.*

FOUNDATION

Listen to the following pieces of music, books, and rhymes, particularly exploring "feeling the difference" through gross motor movement with young singers.

CORE KNOWLEDGE

Lead singers to learn the comparatives by moving, listening to, and purposefully discussing these pairs.

- **fast/slow**

    "Flight of the Bumblebee" from *Tsar Sultan* by Rimsky-Korsakov
    "Berceuse" from *The Firebird* by Stravinsky

- **high/low**

    "Berceuse" from *Eight Russian Folksongs* by Liadov
    "Pantomime" from *The Comedians, Op. 26* by Kabalevsky

- **loud/soft**

    with younger singers read the picture book *Thump, Thump, Rat-a-tat-tat* by Gene Baer, with a steady beat using appropriate dynamics throughout to imitate the approach and passing by of a marching band

    use *The Circus Band March* by Charles Ives with older singers

- **beat divided by 2/beat divided by 3**

    beat divided by 2 nursery rhymes such as *Queen, Queen Caroline*

    > Queen, Queen, Caroline,
    > Washed her hair in turpentine;
    > Turpentine to make it shine,
    > Queen, Queen, Caroline.

    beat divided by 3 nursery rhymes such as *Hickory Dickory Dock*

    > Hickory Dickory Dock,
    > The mouse ran up the clock;
    > The clock struck one,
    > The mouse ran down,
    > Hickory, Dickory Dock.

- **same/different/similar**

    "Sabre Dance" from *Gayenne* by Khachaturian
      FORM: A A¹ B B bridge A A¹ coda
        A versus A = same
        A versus A¹ = similar
        A versus B = different

REHEARSE & ENRICH

1. Teach and compare other pieces of music that you love.
2. Younger singers can use animal voices to explore low and high sounds as well as loud and soft.

> **use of the voice** – *the voice is produced by a group of muscles that can be exercised, strengthened, and used in many ways such as expressing emotions, dynamics, and articulation.*

FOUNDATION

1. Singers memorize a fun rhyme or poem:

   Elementary School – *Grandpa Grig*
   Grandpa Grig had a pig in a field of clover;
   Piggy died, grandpa cried, and all the fun was over.

   Middle School – *Jackanory*
   I'll tell you a story
   About Jack a Nory;
   And now my story's begun;
   I'll tell you another
   Of Jack and his brother,
   And now my story is done.

   High School – *Old King Cole*
   Old King Cole was a merry old soul
   And a merry old soul was he;
   He called for his pipe, and he called for his bowl
   And he called for his fiddlers three.
   Every fiddler he had a fiddle,
   And a very fine fiddle had he;
   Oh there's none so rare, as can compare
   With King Cole and his fiddlers three.

CORE KNOWLEDGE

1. Show four signs with the words **sing, whisper, speak,** and **shout** while singers perform the poems to practice different uses of the voice.

REHEARSE & ENRICH

1. Hold up signs with ***p*** (*piano*), ***m*** (*mezzo*), and ***f*** (*forte*) to explore dynamic use of the voice. Older singers could use all dynamic markings: ***ppp, pp, p, mp, mf, f, ff, fff***, as well as **crescendo** and **diminuendo.**

2. Also use signs with articulation markings (*staccato, legato, portato, marcato, accent, tenuto*, etc.) that will be read from choral octavos during the rehearsal.

3. Have singers create their own poems about using their voices in these ways.

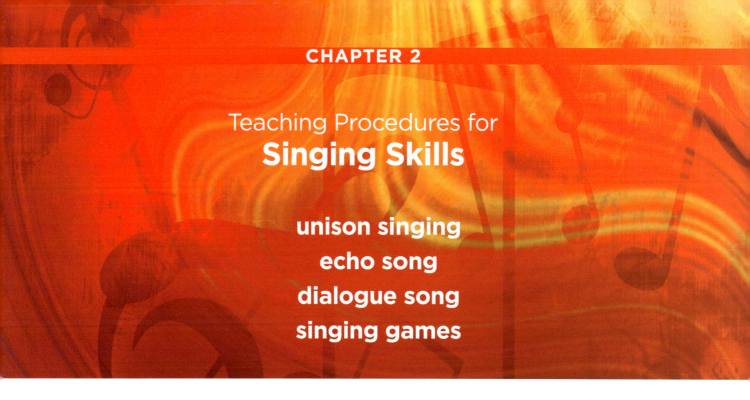

CHAPTER 2

Teaching Procedures for Singing Skills

unison singing
echo song
dialogue song
singing games

unison singing – *simultaneous singing of the same melody at exactly the same pitch.*

ES:	*Twinkle Little Star*
MS:	*Father Grumble*
HS:	*Sweet William*

FOUNDATION

1. Ensemble learns the song through reading or by rote.

CORE KNOWLEDGE

1. **Teacher:** "Everyone sing the same notes at the same time so that you're singing in unison."

2. Teacher points out that while singing in unison, one way to match pitch is through listening to other singers and sing the same thing at the same time with them.

3. Teacher demonstrates both good unison singing and poor unison singing with one singer.

REHEARSE & ENRICH

1. Ensemble sings other unison songs or checks unison sections of part-songs with reminders to listen to the other singers for a unison sound.

2. Older singers can work on singing common vowel sounds to produce unison singing with beautiful blend.

Twinkle Little Star

"The Star" by Jane Taylor, 1806 poem

2. When the blazing sun is gone,
   When he nothing shines upon,
   Then you show your little light,
   Twinkle, twinkle, all the night. (Refrain)

3. Then the traveller in the dark,
   Thanks you for your tiny spark,
   He could not see which way to go,
   If you did not twinkle so. (Refrain)

4. In the dark blue sky you keep,
   And often through my curtains peep,
   For you never shut your eye,
   Till the sun is in the sky. (Refrain)

5. As your bright and tiny spark,
   Lights the traveller in the dark,
   Though I know not what you are,
   Twinkle, twinkle, little star. (Refrain)

Father Grumble

There was an old man that lived in a wood, as you can plain-ly see,

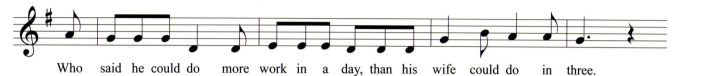
Who said he could do more work in a day, than his wife could do in three.

"If that be so," the old wo-man said, "Why this you must al-low,

That you shall do my work for a day, while I go drive the plough."

2. "But you must milk the tiny cow
   For fear she should go dry
   And you must feed the little pigs
   That are within the sty,
   And you must watch the bracket hen
   Lest she should lay astray,
   And you must wind the reel of yarn
   That I spun yesterday."

3. The old woman took the staff in her hand
   And went to drive the plough;
   The old man took the pail in his hand
   And went to milk the cow;
   But Tiny hitched and Tiny flinched
   And Tiny cocked her nose
   And Tiny hit the old man such a kick
   That the blood ran down to his toes.

4. 'T'was, "Hey, my good cow," and "How, my good
   cow," And "Now, my good cow, stand still.
   If ever I milk this cow again,
   'Twill be against my will."
   And when he'd milked the tiny cow
   For fear she should go dry,
   Why, then he fed the little pigs
   That were within the sty.

5. And then he watched the bracket hen,
   Lest she should lay astray,
   But he forgot the reel of yarn
   His wife spun yesterday.
   He swore by all the leaves on the tree,
   And all the stars in heaven,
   That his wife could do more work in a day
   Than he could do in seven.

Sweet William

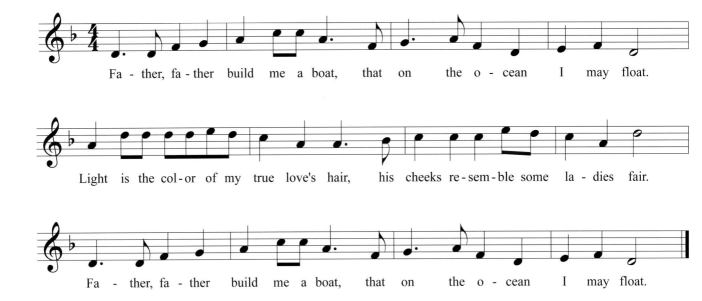

echo song – *song in which each phrase sung by a group or soloist is repeated (echoed) exactly by another group or soloist.*

ES: *Johnny On a Woodpile*
MS: *Tongo*
HS: *Ol' Texas*

SONG PREPARATION

1. Use warm-ups where the conductor gives the ensemble a cue to sing without counting off or giving verbal directions to sing; use gesture only.

FOUNDATION

1. Teacher demonstrates, "sh, sh, sh, sh" and gestures to ensemble to echo, "sh, sh, sh, sh."
2. Teacher demonstrates, "du, du, du, du" and gestures to ensemble to echo, "du, du, du, du."
3. Teacher continues using consonants appropriate to the song being sung such as "j, j, j, j" for *Johnny on the Woodpile,* "t, g, t, g" for *Tongo,* or "t, t, t, t" for *Ol' Texas*.

CORE KNOWLEDGE

1. Teacher directs, "I'll sing some musical phrases and you copy me exactly when I cue you with my hands."
2. Teacher sings first motif and gives ensemble a cue to echo; ensemble echoes.
3. Continue with the entire song.
4. Ensemble practices a few times through until the song is fluid.
5. *Teacher:* "An echo works when a person stands at a canyon's edge and speaks, it echoes – repeats – back to her and she hears herself say the exact same thing."
6. *Teacher:* "Because your singing copies my singing exactly, this is called an echo song."

REHEARSE & ENRICH

1. Sing other echo songs and once they are well-known use ensemble members as leaders.
2. Eventually compare echo songs (echo is exactly the same as the call) with call & response songs (response has either a melodic or rhythmic difference from the call).

Johnny On A Woodpile

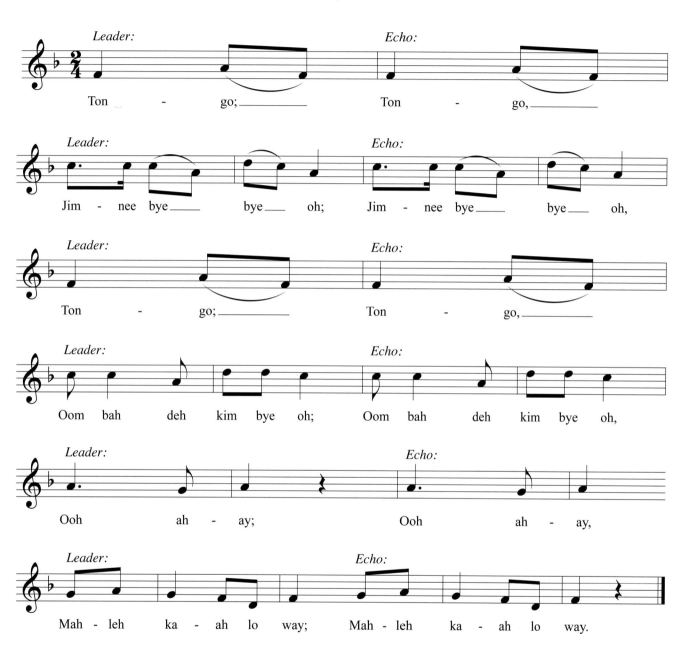

This Polynesian text is transliterated (written in English sound-alike syllables rather than an actual language) so pronounce as written.

Ol' Texas

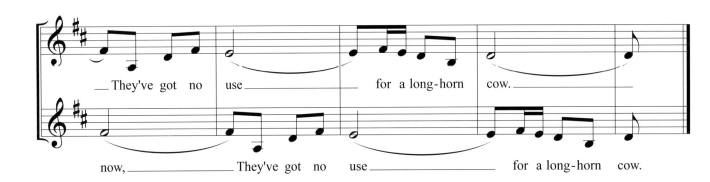

2. They've plowed and fenced my cattle range,
   And the people there are all so strange.

3. I'll take my horse, I'll take my rope,
   And hit the trail upon a lope.

4. Say adios to the Alamo
   And hit the trail toward Mexico.

dialogue song – *a song that depicts a conversation between two people.*

ES: *There's A Hole in the Bucket*
MS: *My Good Old Man*
HS: *Buffalo Boy* (accompany with guitar or banjo)

SONG PREPARATION

1. Ensemble learns the song through reading or by rote.

FOUNDATION

1. Teacher asks "What day of the week is today?" Ensemble responds.

2. Teacher asks "What color are your shoes?" Individuals respond.

3. *Teacher:* "A conversation (talking) between two people is referred to as a dialogue."

CORE KNOWLEDGE

1. Ensemble sings the entire song in unison.

2. Teacher leads discussion on who is speaking to whom in each verse (man versus woman).

3. *Teacher:* "A song that carries on a conversation between two people is called a dialogue song."

4. Ensemble sings the song in two parts: men versus women (a.k.a. boys versus girls).

REHEARSE & ENRICH

1. Simple gestures or costumes for each dialogue group, or one man and one woman at the front of the stage in pantomime create a concert audience pleaser.

There's A Hole in the Bucket

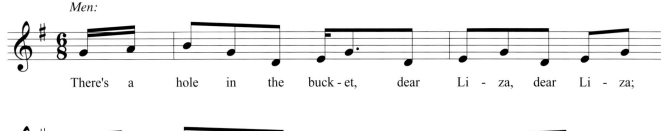

Women: Then fix it, dear Henry, dear Henry, dear Henry;
Then fix it, dear Henry, dear Henry, fix it.

Men: With what shall I fix it, dear Liza…
Women: With a straw, dear Henry…
Men: But the straw is too long, dear Liza…
Women: Then cut it, dear Henry…
Men: With what shall I cut it, dear Liza…
Women: With an axe, dear Henry…
Men: The axe is too dull, dear Liza…
Women: Then sharpen it, dear Henry…
Men: With what shall I sharpen it, dear Liza…
Women: With a stone, dear Henry…
Men: The stone is too dry, dear Liza…
Women: Then wet it, dear Henry…
Men: With what shall I wet it, dear Liza…
Women: With water, dear Henry…
Men: How shall I get water, dear Liza…
Women: In the bucket, dear Henry…
Men: There's a hole in the bucket, dear Liza…

My Good Old Man

Women sing the verses and men give the spoken reply in dialogue.

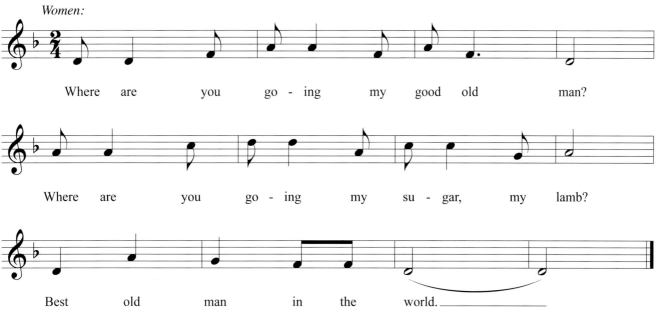

2. What will you buy there, my good old man?
   What will you buy there, my sugar, my lamb?
   Best old man in the world.
   (Spoken) Bushel of eggs.

3. Bushel will kill you, my good old man,
   Bushel will kill you, my sugar, my lamb,
   Best old man in the world,
   (Spoken) Don't care if it does.

4. What for to die, my good old man?
   What for to die, my sugar, my lamb?
   Best old man in the world.
   (Spoken) So I can haunt you.

5. Why will you haunt me, my good old man?
   Why will you haunt me, my sugar, my lamb?
   Best old man in the world.
   (Spoken) So I can always be near you.

Buffalo Boy

Women sing the odd numbered verses and men sing the even numbered verses in dialogue.

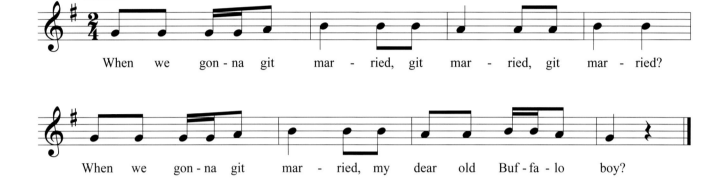

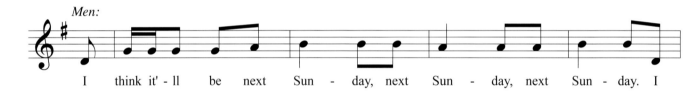

3. What will you wear to the wedding?, etc.
   My dear old Buffalo Boy?

4. I think I'll wear my overalls, etc.
   That is if the weather be good.

5. What will you drive to the wedding?, etc.
   My dear old Buffalo Boy?

6. I think I'll drive my ox cart, etc.
   That is if the weather be good.

7. Why don't you come in the buggy?, etc.
   My dear old Buffalo boy?

8. My mule won't take to the buggy, etc.
   Not even if the weather be good.

9. Who will you bring to the wedding?, etc.
   My dear old Buffalo Boy?

10. I think I'll bring my children, etc.
    That is if the weather be good.

11. I didn't know you had children, etc.
    My dear old Buffalo Boy.

12. Oh, yes, I have five children, etc.
    And six, if the weather be good.

13. There ain't gonna be no wedding, etc.
    My dear old Buffalo Boy!

singing games – *games in which the accompanying music is sung by the participants with the game played by adhering to the text of the song that often includes motions, actions, or competitive rules.*

To the teacher: singing game participants often have to perform multiple tasks at once such as singing, holding hands, walking, and choosing another person, making singing games a wonderful way to introduce part-work skills.

Games can be used for times of relaxation or revitalization of energy during any rehearsal or class.

- **ES:** *The Farmer in the Dell*
- **MS:** *Dance Josey*
- **HS:** *Turn the Glasses Over*

SONG PREPARATION

1. Younger singers learn the game and the song simultaneously as the teacher directs the playing of the game.
2. Older singers can learn the song through reading or by rote before playing the game.

FOUNDATION

1. Ensemble sings the game song and keeps the beat in their feet in a stationary position or by patting on their legs.

CORE KNOWLEDGE

1. Play games according to the directions encouraging students to sing well while performing the motions/actions of the game.

REHEARSE & ENRICH

1. Play the same game multiple times over the course of a semester so that the singers can play self-directed (no help from the teacher).

The Farmer in the Dell

2. The farmer takes a wife...

3. The wife takes a child...

4. The child takes a nurse...

5. The nurse takes a cow...

6. The cow takes a dog...

7. The dog takes a cat...

8. The cat takes a rat...

9. The rat takes the cheese...

10. The cheese stands alone...

The Farmer in the Dell

GAME DIRECTIONS

The players form a circle holding hands around one who is designated as the farmer, singing the first verse while moving around the circle. By the time the verse is over, the farmer makes his choice of a wife.

The wife joins the farmer in the center for her verse then makes her choice of the child and so on through the verses until the cheese is selected.

At this point, all of those in the middle rejoin the circle except for the cheese who stands in the middle of the circle. Everyone stands in place, claps the beat, and sings the last verse to the sole child in the center.

The cheese becomes the farmer for the next round.

Dance Josey

2. Chewing my gum so I can't dance Josey, (Sing 3 times)
   Hello Susan Browny-o.

3. Shoestring's broke so I can't dance Josey (Sing 3 times)
   Hello Susan Browny-o.

4. Holding my mule so I can't dance Josey, (Sing 3 times)
   Hello Susan Browny-o.

5. Hair in the butter so I can't dance Josey, (Sing 3 times)
   Hello Susan Browny-o.

6. Briar in my heels so I can't dance Josey, (Sing 3 times)
   Hello Susan Browny-o.

7. Stumped my toe so I can't dance Josey, (Sing 3 times)
   Hello Susan Browny-o.

Improvise more verses as to why you can't dance....

Dance Josey

GAME DIRECTIONS

Students stand in two concentric circles holding hands. Teacher places a rubber chicken in the middle of the inner circle, then steps in between the two circles.

Two students are chosen to be "foxes" who will try to get the chicken. The foxes stand away from the group, turn their backs to the circle and hide their eyes while the class sings the song.

During the song, the outer circle walks to the beat, moving to the left while the inner circle walks to the beat, moving to right. The teacher taps one set of held hands in each circle while the song is sung, then moves to the outside of the circle.

Upon singing of the last three syllables of the song ("Brown-y-o"), the pairs of students tapped by the teacher in both circles raise their arms to create a gate in the fences around the chicken. At the same time, the circles of students stops walking and the two foxes must enter through each gate, racing towards the center of the middle circle.

The first fox to get the chicken wins the game.

With very large groups, multiple concentric circles may be used.

Turn the Glasses Over

I've been to Har-lem, I've been to Do-ver, I've trav-elled this wide world all o-ver,
o-ver, o-ver, three times o-ver, Drink all the bran-dy wine, and turn the glass-es o-ver.
Sail-ing east, sail-ing west, Sail-ing o'er the o-cean,
Bet-ter watch out when the boat be-gins to rock, Or you'll lose your girl in the o-cean.

Turn the Glasses Over

GAME DIRECTIONS

One child stands in the midle of a circle of partners who promenade around the circle during the first seven measures.

On "turn the glasses over", the partner on the outside turns under the inside partner's arms, changing direction. Partners let go.

The inside and outside circles walk the beat in opposite directions until "lose your girl in the ocean" - this last syllable is spoken with vigor, and the child in the middle rushes with everyone from the inside circle to find a partner from the outside circle, thus leaving one child without a partner.

This singer is now "it" in the middle and the game begins anew.

CHAPTER 3

Teaching Procedures for
Rhythmic Part-work Skills
(Intersperse with Rhythmic Part-work Skills)

beat

beat while stationary
beat through locomotor movement
beat through body ostinato

beat division

beat versus beat division

rhythm

beat versus beat division versus rhythm

rhythmic ostinato

multiple rhythmic ostinati

rhythm canon

rhythm body canon

beat – *physically keeping the steady pulse to music while stationary, through locomotor movement, or with a body ostinato.*

SONG PREPARATION

1. Review songs and rhymes previously learned in this sequence.

FOUNDATION

1. Singers sing songs and say rhymes in unison without the teacher's help.

CORE KNOWLEDGE – *beat while stationary*

1. Singers perform a song or rhyme that is well known.
2. Teacher directs, "You perform again while I do something different."
3. Singers perform the song or rhyme while the teacher keeps the beat by tapping her hand over her heart.
4. *Teacher:* "I am keeping the steady pulse to this song/rhyme called the beat."
5. Teacher instructs, "Copy my motions to keep the beat as you perform this song/rhyme."
6. Singers perform the song or rhyme and keep the beat by tapping a hand over their hearts.
7. *Teacher:* "Beat is the steady pulse to music. Our body can keep the beat to music in multiple ways."
8. Singers perform the song or rhyme and practice the beat by tapping their legs, clapping their hands, or by playing unpitched rhythm instruments while sitting in seats/standing in one spot. Older singers can do these activities to recordings of complex, interesting music.

REHEARSE & ENRICH

beat through locomotor movement – first, young singers walk the beat as they stay in place, then walk the beat as they travel around the room. Older singers should move to the beat forward, backward, sideways, diagonally, etc.

beat through body ostinato – younger singers perform an ostinato on their bodies such as tapping their heads for two beats and then tapping their shoulders for two beats creating a body ostinato. Older singers can create a body ostinato that is more challenging wherein they cross arms, alternate upper and lower parts of the body, or that are eight beats long.

beat division – *physically keeping the beat division (whether the beat is divided by 2 or 3 sounds) while singing or listening to music.*

SONG PREPARATION

1. Review songs and rhymes previously learned in this sequence.

FOUNDATION

1. Singers sing songs and say rhymes in unison without the teacher's help.

CORE KNOWLEDGE

1. Singers perform a song or rhyme that is well known and keep the beat.

2. Teacher directs, "You perform and keep the beat again while I do something different."

3. Singers perform the song or rhyme while the teacher keeps the beat division by tapping on her legs.

4. *Teacher:* "I am keeping the sound that goes faster than the beat to this song/rhyme called the beat division."

5. Teacher instructs, "Copy my motions to keep the beat division as you perform this song/rhyme."

6. Singers perform the song or rhyme and keep the beat division by tapping on their legs.

7. *Teacher:* "Beat is the steady pulse to music, the beat can be divided. Our body can keep the beat division to music in multiple ways."

8. Singers perform the song or rhyme and practice the beat division by tapping their heads, clapping their hands, or by playing unpitched rhythm instruments. Older singers can do these activities to recordings of complex, interesting music.

REHEARSE & ENRICH

beat divided by 2 – singers march to a familiar song or rhyme with the beat divided by 2 sounds. **Teacher:** "When the beat marches it is divided by two sounds, so the beat name is "ta" and the beat division name is "ta-ti."

beat divided by 3 – singers swing their arms or imaginary skate to a familiar song or rhyme with the beat divided by 3 sounds. **Teacher:** "When the beat swings it is divided by three sounds, so the beat name is "ta" and the beat division name is "ta-tu-te."

beat versus beat division via ensemble – half of the singers keep the beat while the other half simultaneously keeps the beat division as they all sing the song in unison.

beat versus beat division via individual – older singers can be asked to keep the beat in one part of their body and tap the beat division on another part in many creative ways such as walking the beat and tapping the beat division on thighs. This is especially beneficial to those singers who have a high musical aptitude and need the extra challenge.

> **rhythm** – *rhythm is how many sounds are produced on each beat by the text. Rhythm can match the beat, match the beat division, or be different than either the beat or beat division.*

SONG PREPARATION

1. Review songs and rhymes previously learned in this sequence.

FOUNDATION

1. Singers sing songs and say rhymes in unison without the teacher's help.

CORE KNOWLEDGE

1. Singers perform a song or rhyme that is well known and keep the beat.

2. Teacher directs, "You perform and keep the beat again while I do something different."

3. Singers perform the song or rhyme while the teacher claps the words by tapping one hand lightly into her other hand directly in front of her mouth.

4. Singers identify that the teacher was clapping the way the words go (older students identify that the teacher was clapping the text).

5. **Teacher:** "The way the words go is called rhythm."
6. Teacher instructs, "Perform the rhythm by clapping your hands in front of your mouth to catch each part of every word."
7. Singers perform the song or rhyme and clap the rhythm.

REHEARSE & ENRICH

beat versus rhythm via ensemble – half of the singers keep the beat while the other half simultaneously clap the rhythm as they all sing the song in unison.

beat versus rhythm via individual – older singers can be asked to keep the beat in one part of their body and tap the rhythm on another part in many creative ways such as walking the beat and tapping the rhythm on their shoulders (arms crossed over chest). This is especially beneficial to those singers who have a high musical aptitude and need the extra challenge.

beat versus beat division versus rhythm via ensemble – the ensemble can be divided into thirds with one group marching the beat, a second group tapping the beat division, and the third group clapping the rhythm while the entire ensemble is singing the song in unison.

beat versus beat division verses rhythm via individual - old singers can keep the beat in one foot, the beat division in the other foot, and clap the rhythm.

rhythmic ostinato – *a rhythm pattern that is repeated throughout a piece of music.*

    ES: *Hill and Gully Rider*
    MS: *Come, Let Us All A-Maying Go*
    HS: *Chantey*

SONG PREPARATION

1. Ensemble practices the song until members can sing the first verse from memory without help from the teacher.

FOUNDATION

1. Teacher claps multiple 4- or 6- beat rhythm patterns (depending on the song choice) with ensemble clapping back and saying the rhythm syllables. Teacher must repeat ONE of the patterns intermittently throughout the warm-up (which is actually the ostinato for the song). At the end of clapping exercise, ensemble derives which pattern was clapped multiple times. The teacher writes this rhythm pattern on the board.

CORE KNOWLEDGE

1. Ensemble sings the song without help from the teacher.

2. Ensemble reads the rhythm pattern from the board in rhythm syllables; singers practice until it is memorized.

3. $2/3$ ensemble sings song versus $1/3$ ensemble claps the ostinato at the same time.

4. Take turns until all sections of the ensemble have performed both parts.

5. **Teacher:** "This repeated pattern is an ostinato, but because it's not melodious we identify it more specifically as a rhythmic ostinato."

REHEARSE & ENRICH

1. Encourage the ensemble members to each create their own ostinato – the motif can be taken directly from the song (complimentary ostinato) or made up differently than the song (contrary ostinato).

2. Perform multiple rhythmic ostinati at the same time with the tune.

3. Perform each rhythmic ostinato on a different rhythm instrument.

4. Ensemble members can create text to match each rhythmic ostinato as appropriate to the tune.

5. Sing a canon in parts and add multiple rhythmic ostinati for an excellent practice of small groups holding their own part against others.

6. High school singers can perform difficult ostinati within the first few examples.

Hill and Gully Rider

2. Oh the moon shine bright down, hill and gully.
   Ain't no place to hide and down, hill and gully,
   And a zombie come a-riding, down hill and gully. (Refrain)

3. Oh my knees they shake down, hill and gully,
   And my heart starts quaking down, hill and gully,
   And I run 'til daylight breaking down, hill and gully. (Refrain)

4. That's the last I set down, hill and gully.
   Pray the Lord don't let me down, hill and gully.
   Ain't nobody gonna get me down, hill and gully. (Refrain)

Come, Let Us All A-Maying Go

John Hilton

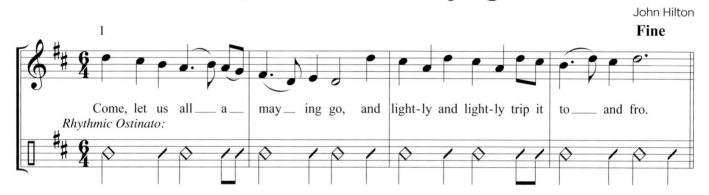

This tune can also be sung in canon with entrances at 1, 2, 3.

Chantey

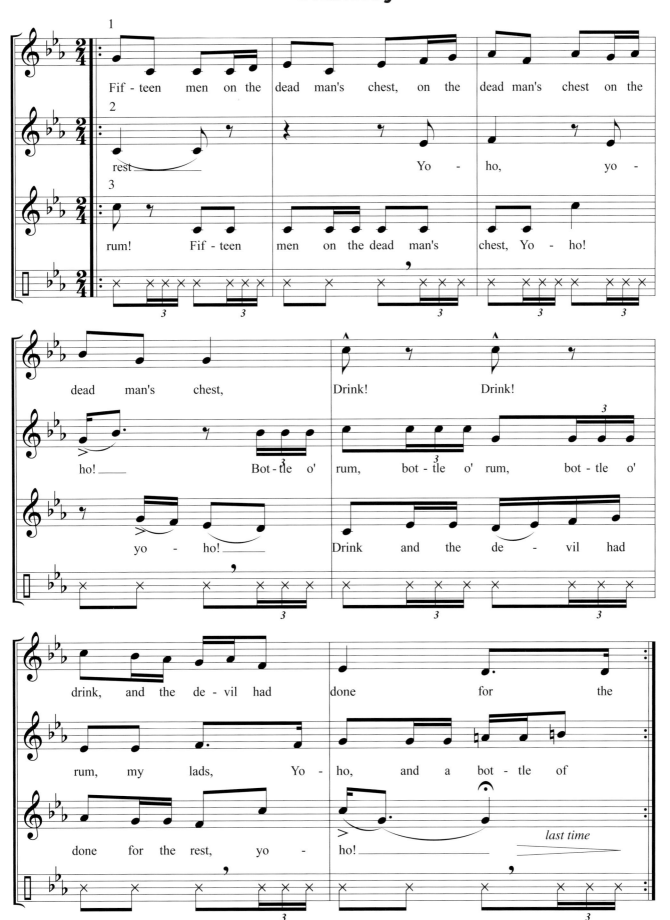

One Accord • Developing Part-Singing Skills in School-Age Musicians

multiple rhythmic ostinati – *two or more rhythmic ostinatos performed simultaneously.*

ES/MS/HS: *Twinkle Little Star + Rhythmic Ostinati*

Ensemble practices clapping the first ostinato, then practices tapping the second on their legs. The singers then take turns singing the words of the song or performing one ostinato.

Divide the ensemble into three sections, this time having one group clap the first ostinato, the second group tap the second ostinato on their legs, and the third group sing the song. With practice, the singers will get to the point where they can all perform the song while half of the class claps ostinato one and the other half taps ostinato two. Eventually the singers will be able to individually sing the song and clap an ostinato at the same time.

Encourage singers to volunteer to perform duets like this for the ensemble. As a musical challenge the ensemble could sing the rhythm syllables of the song instead of the words.

Twinkle Little Star + Rhythmic Ostinati

"The Star" by Jane Taylor, 1806 poem

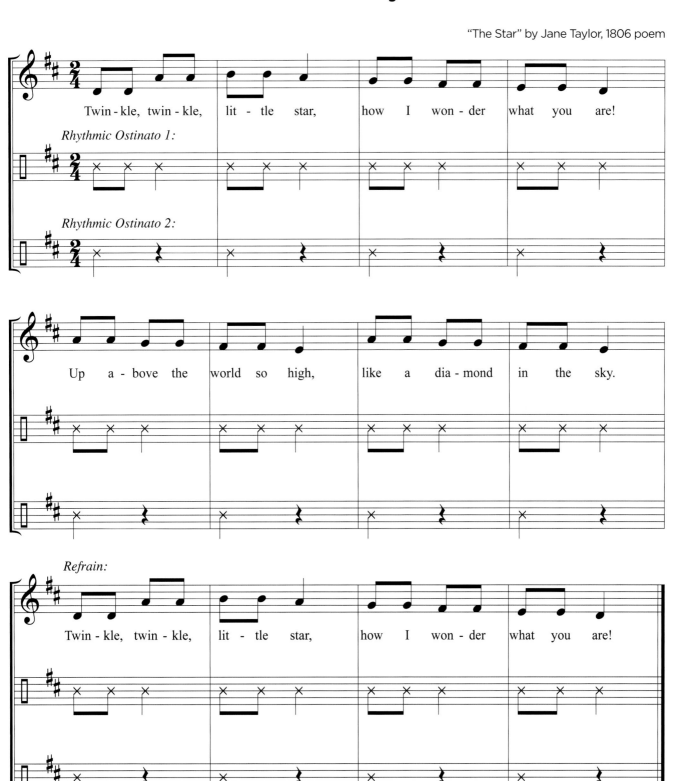

rhythm canon – *performing a song as the rhythm is clapped in canon.*

In the beginning, the ensemble will sing the rhythm syllables to a song as the teacher claps in canon. Next, the ensemble will be divided in half, with one half singing the song in rhythm syllables as the other half claps in canon.

In due course, the singers should have enough practice so that they can sing the rhythm syllables to the song and clap in canon with themselves. This activity could be done by having the rhythm written on the board for them to read, then eventually having both parts performed without visual aid.

If this is the first time students have clapped in canon, use the easier version in which the rhythm of the clapping is the same rhythm that is being sung. The concept of rhythm canon is new but the skill level is easy. With practice, these students can eventually move to the challenging version.

If the students have previously mastered the skill of clapping in canon, use the challenging version in which the rhythm of the clapping is contrary to the rhythm of the singing. This skill level challenges more experienced musicians.

ES/MS/HS: *Twinkle Little Star – Easier Version*
Twinkle Little Star – Challenging Version

rhythm body canon – *instead of clapping in canon, assign each rhythmic element to a specific body part.*

Once singers can sing the song and clap in canon with themselves, another step of difficulty can be added such as:

- quarter note equals tapping one foot on the floor
- eighth notes equals tapping on the head.

Have singers perform the song with rhythm names, while simultaneously performing these motions, then have half of the class chant the rhythm syllables while the other half performs the motions in canon.

Similarly, half of the ensemble can sing the words to a known song while the other half of the ensemble performs the body motions in canon.

After practicing this skill with a number of songs, challenge the singers to sing the words of a song while performing the body motions in canon with themselves. Singers love the opportunity to show off these body canon skills to the ensemble.

ES/MS/HS: *Twinkle Little Star – Easier Version*
Twinkle Little Star – Challenging Version

Twinkle Little Star + Rhythm Canon
Easier Version

"The Star" by Jane Taylor, 1806 poem

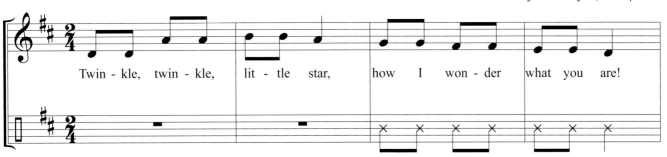

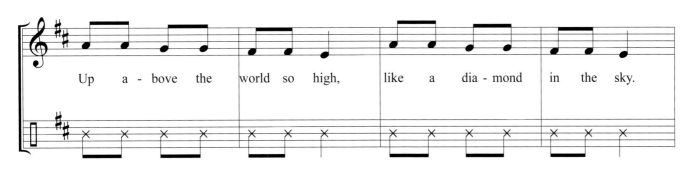

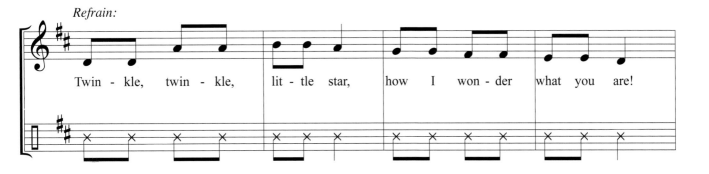

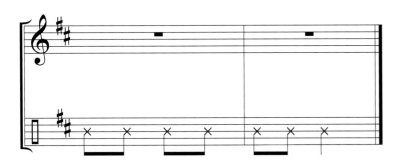

Twinkle Little Star + Rhythm Canon
Challenging Version

"The Star" by Jane Taylor, 1806 poem

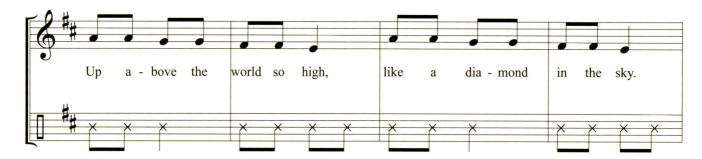

Refrain:

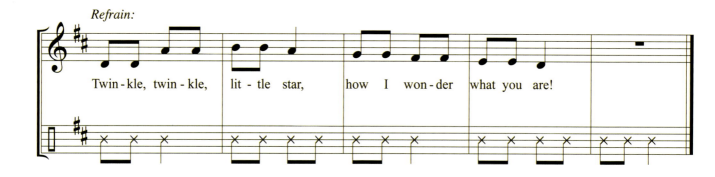

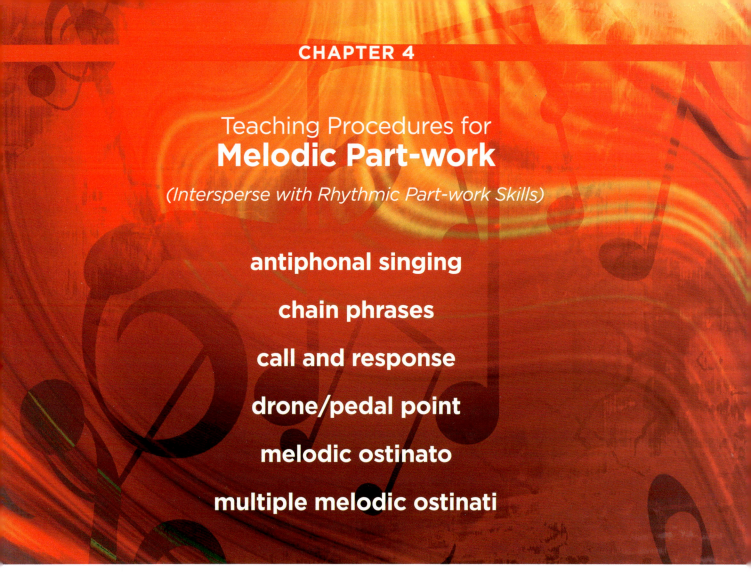

CHAPTER 4

Teaching Procedures for Melodic Part-work

(Intersperse with Rhythmic Part-work Skills)

- antiphonal singing
- chain phrases
- call and response
- drone/pedal point
- melodic ostinato
- multiple melodic ostinati

antiphonal singing – *small groups of singers each sing one phrase of a song without stopping between phrases.*

Referred to as chain phrases when each phrase is sung by an individual rather than a group of singers.

- **ES:** *Who's That?*
- **MS:** *Lavender's Blue*
- **HS:** *God Bless the Moon*

SONG PREPARATION

1. Ensemble sings the song in unison for a number of class periods until it is well known, including small group and solo singing.

FOUNDATION

1. Teacher instructs, "See if you can hear the phrases of this song in your head – audiate – without singing them. I'll sing the first phrase and when I gesture a cue, you mouth the second phrase. Be careful not to whisper or sing, just mouth the words and hear the song in your head." (Older students need not mouth the text, just audiate the song).

2. Teacher sings the first phrase of the song, ensemble mouths the second phrase of the song while they audiate the song.

3. Teacher sings the third phrase of the song, ensemble mouths the forth phrase of the song, continuing to the end of the song.

CORE KNOWLEDGE

1. Once the song is known well, the ensemble sings it through one time.

2. Teacher says, "When I show my arms around your section (cue) you sing, when I show my arms around another section (cue) of the ensemble they will sing and you hear the song inside your head."

3. First half of the ensemble sings phrase 1, the second half of the ensemble sings phrase 2; the first half of the ensemble sings phrase 3, the second half of the ensemble sings phrase 4; continuing to the end of the song.

4. **Teacher:** "When part of the ensemble sings a phrase and another part of the ensemble sings a corresponding phrase, it's called antiphonal singing."

5. Teacher directs the group again, switching phrases from step 3.

REHEARSE & ENRICH

1. Sing other songs by dividing the ensemble into 2-parts, then 3-, 4-, or more parts with each group singing one phrase of each given tune.

2. Continue until the singers are singing each phrase as a soloist. At this point the term is chain phrases.

3. Play recordings for the ensemble through a stereo system in which the singers can clearly hear the sound moving from one speaker to the other antiphonally.

4. For older singers you could briefly speak about Domenico Gabrielli who used the unusual layout of the San Marco church, with its two choir lofts facing each other, to create striking musical effects. Most of his pieces were written so that a choir or instrumental ensemble would first be heard on one side, then was followed by a response from the musicians on the other side. Play recordings of Gabrielli's music through stereo speakers so the singers hear the antiphonal effect.

Who's That?

Lavender's Blue

2. Call up your men, dilly, dilly, set them to work.
   Some with a hoe, dilly, dilly, some with a fork;
   Some to pitch hay, dilly, dilly, some to hoe corn,
   While you and I, dilly, dilly, keep ourselves warm.

3. Lavender's green, dilly, dilly, lavender's blue,
   If you love me, dilly, dilly, I will love you.
   Hear the bird sing, dilly, dilly, see the lambs play;
   We shall be safe, dilly, dilly, out of harm's way.

God Bless the Moon

> **chain phrases** – *individual singers sing one phrase of a song in succession without stopping between phrases; also known as relay singing.*

Referred to as antiphonal singing when phrases are sung by groups of singers rather than individuals.

- **ES:** *Sea Shell*
- **MS:** *Tom Dooley*
- **HS:** *Sakura*

SONG PREPARATION

1. The ensemble learns the song through sight reading or by rote.

FOUNDATION

1. Teacher instructs, "I'll sing the first phrase of a song and when I gesture a cue, you all sing the second phrase."
2. Teacher sings the first phrase of the song, ensemble sings the second phrase of the song.
3. Teacher sings the third phrase of the song, ensemble sings the forth phrase of the song, continuing to the end of the song.

CORE KNOWLEDGE

1. Sing the song by dividing the ensemble into 2-parts, then 3-, 4-, or more parts with each group singing one phrase of each given tune.
2. Continue until the singers are singing each phrase as a soloist.
3. **Teacher:** "We are singing chain phrases – just like antiphonal singing, but with individual singers singing each phrase as a soloist."

REHEARSE & ENRICH

1. Play recordings of an a cappella choral ensemble through a stereo system in which the singers can clearly hear the sound moving from one singer to another.

Sea Shell

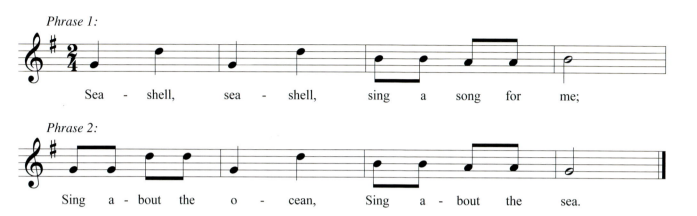

Tom Dooley

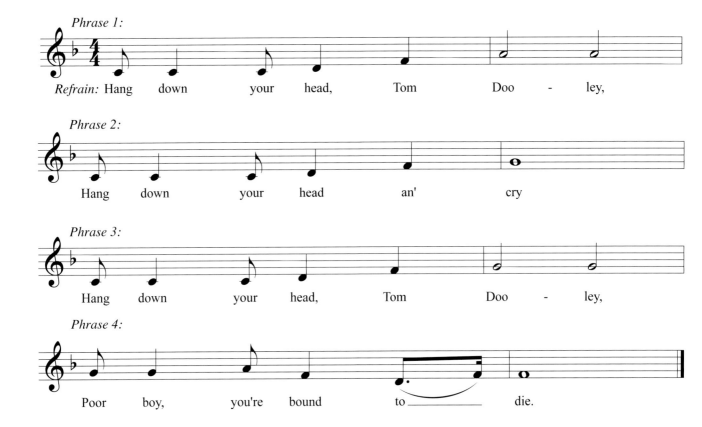

1. Hang down your head, Tom Dooley,
   Hang down your head and cry.
   Killed little Laurie Foster,
   Poor boy, you're bound to die. (Refrain)

2. I met her on the mountain,
   There I took her life.
   I met her on the mountain,
   Stabbed her with my knife. (Refrain)

3. Hand me down my banjo,
   I'll pick it on my knee.
   By this time tomorrow
   It'll be no use to me. (Refrain)

4. By this time tomorrow,
   Reckon where I'll be.
   If it hadn't been for Grayson,
   I'd have been in Tennessee. (Refrain)

5. By this time tomorrow,
   Reckon where I'll be.
   Down in some lonesome valley,
   Hanging from a white oak tree. (Refrain)

Sakura

Japanese (in transliteration)

This Japanese text is transliterated (written in English sound-alike syllables rather than an actual language) so pronounce as written with vowels sounding:

a = [a] as in olive   **i** = [i] as is in green   **o** = [o] as in gold   **u** = [u] as in blue

call and response – *song in which each phrase sung by a group or soloist (call) is answered by another group or soloist with a motif or phrase that is not the same as the call (response).*

Singing that alternates between a soloist (call) and a congregation (response) in liturgical situations is referred to as responsorial singing.

> **ES:** *John the Rabbit*
> **MS:** *Sail Away Ladies*
> **HS:** *The Devil's Nine Questions*

SONG PREPARATION

1. Teacher sings the entire song for the ensemble for them to hear the form.

FOUNDATION

1. Teacher sings "Yoo-hoo" in various places in the voice and instructs the singers to echo.

2. Teacher sings "Anybody home?" Singers reply by singing "Yoo-hoo".

3. Teacher sings "Are you there?" Singers reply by singing "Yoo-hoo".

CORE KNOWLEDGE

1. Teacher instructs the ensemble to "Echo me." Teacher sings only the response of the song and the ensemble echoes it – practice until the response is known.

2. Teacher directs, "This time I will sing something different, but you continue to sing the same response that you just learned when I cue you."

3. Teacher sings the first call then cues singers to sing the response in time.

4. **Teacher:** "I'm giving a call and you're answering with a response. This style of song is call and response. I sing the call but your answer, the response, is not the same as the call."

5. Sing the entire song with teacher singing all of the calls and the singers singing the response.

REHEARSE & ENRICH

1. Sing other call and response songs then have small groups, duets, or soloists sing the response.

2. When the songs are well known, individual singers take turns being the caller.

John the Rabbit

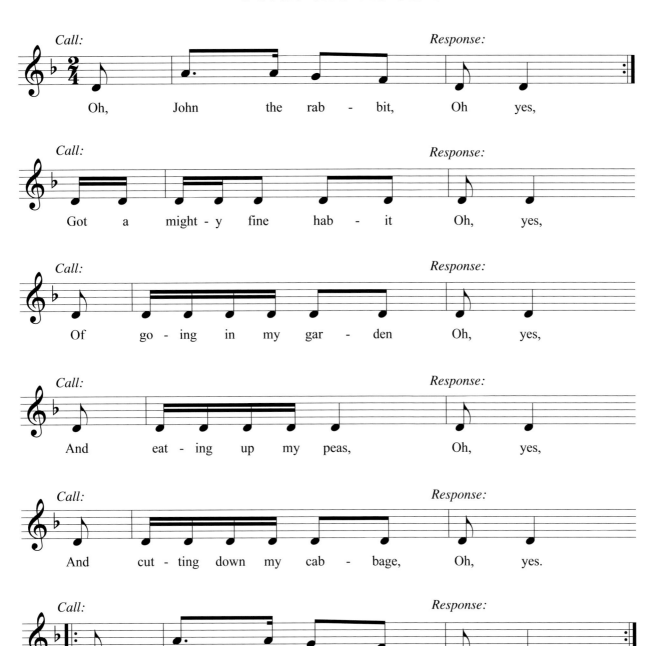

Melody continued on p. 58 >

John the Rabbit *continued*

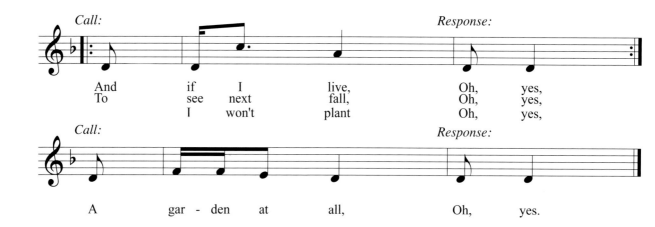

Sail Away Ladies

2. I've got a home in Tennessee, Sail away, ladies, sail away.
   That's the place I wanna be, Sail away, ladies, sail away. (Refrain)

3. If ever I get my new house done, Sail away, ladies, sail away.
   I'll give the old one to my son, Sail away, ladies, sail away. (Refrain)

4. Come along boys, and go with me, Sail away, ladies, sail away.
   We'll go down to Tennessee, Sail away, ladies, sail away. (Refrain)

5. Ever I get my new house done, Sail away, ladies, sail away.
   Love you pretty girls, one by one, Sail away, ladies, sail away. (Refrain)

6. Hush little baby, don't you cry, Sail away, ladies, sail away.
   You'll be an angel by and by, Sail away, ladies, sail away. (Refrain)

The Devil's Nine Questions

2. Oh, what is higher than the tree?
   And what is deeper than the sea?

3. Oh, heaven is higher than the tree,
   And love is deeper than the sea.

4. Oh, what is whiter than the milk?...
   And what is softer than the silk?...

5. Oh, snow is whiter than the milk,...
   And down is softer than the silk....

6. Oh, what is louder than the horn?...
   And what is sharper than the thorn?...

7. Oh, thunder's louder than the horn,...
   And hunger's sharper than the thorn....

8. Oh, what is heavier than the lead?...
   And what is better than the bread?...

9. Oh, grief is heavier than the lead,...
   God's blessing better than the bread....

10. Now you have answered my questions nine,...
    Oh, you are God's, you're none of mine....

The responses remain the same for all verses. If all eight questions are answered correctly you belong to God, so the Devil's ninth question is already answered: "Are you God's or are you mine?"

[drone – *sustained tone(s), usually lower than the melody.*

Also referred to as pedal point because on the organ, the drone is generally played on the pedals.

- **ES:** *Bow Wow Wow*
- **MS:** *Great Big House*
- **HS:** *Ah, Poor Bird*

SONG PREPARATION

1. Ensemble learns the song in the folk tradition.

FOUNDATION

1. Ensemble can sing the folk song from memory without help from the teacher.

CORE KNOWLEDGE – *younger students*

1. Ensemble sings the song with no help from the teacher.
2. Teacher instructs, "You sing the song again but this time I will do something different as you sing."
3. Ensemble sings song while teacher sings the drone.
4. Teacher says, "I'll sing my part repeatedly, once you have listened and know it, sing with me."
5. Ensemble members practice until they can sing the drone without teacher help.
6. *Teacher:* "I will sing the song as the ensemble sings the drone."
7. Singers derive the characteristics of a drone (same pitch or pitches are repeated or held).

CORE KNOWLEDGE – *older students*

1. Ensemble reads the drone from the board in rhythm and solfège.
2. ½ ensemble sings the song versus ½ ensemble sings the drone; switch parts.
3. Singers derive the characteristics of a drone (same pitch is repeated or held) and teacher identifies it as a drone.

REHEARSE & ENRICH

1. Drones can also be played on instruments.
2. The drone is usually based on the tonic or tonic/dominant notes.

Bow Wow Wow

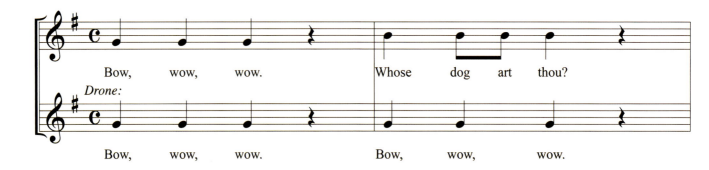

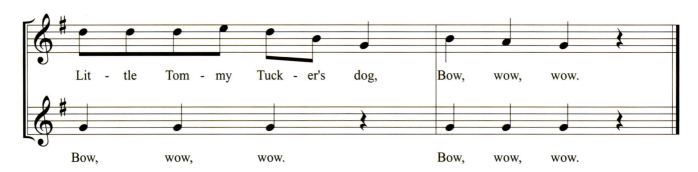

Great Big House

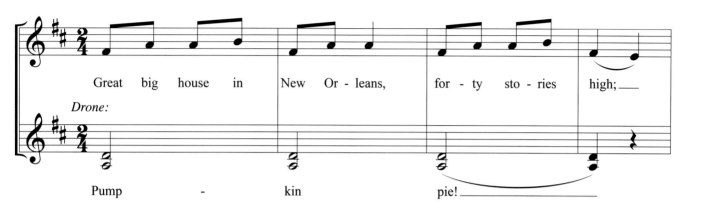

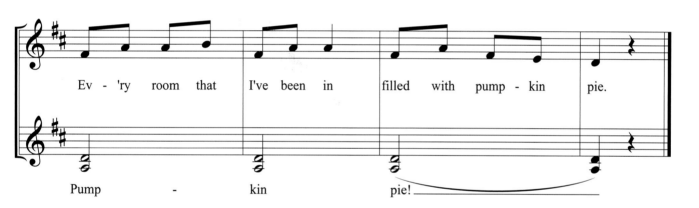

2. Went down to the old mill stream to fetch a pail of water,
   Put one arm around my wife, the other 'round my daughter.

3. Fare thee well my darlin' girl, fare thee well my daughter,
   Fare thee well my darlin' girl with the golden slippers on her.

Ah, Poor Bird

English, German

The Temple Choir songbook, 1871

This tune can also be sung in canon with entrances at 1, 2, 3, 4.

melodic ostinato – a motif (short succession of notes) that is repeated at the same pitch throughout a piece of music.

ES: *Skin and Bones*
MS: *Rocky Mountain*
HS: *Ol' Joe Clark*

SONG PREPARATION

1. Ensemble learns the song in the folk tradition.

FOUNDATION

1. Ensemble can sing the folk song from memory without help from the teacher.

CORE KNOWLEDGE

1. Ensemble sings the song without help from the teacher.

2. Ensemble reads the ostinato from the board through rhythm names and solfège, then practices until known.

3. **Teacher:** "The little section of music that is repeated is called a motif (short succession of notes), and when a motif is repeated throughout a piece of music it is called a melodic ostinato."

4. $2/3$ ensemble sings song versus $1/3$ ensemble sings the ostinato at the same time.

5. Take turns until all sections of the ensemble have sung both parts.

REHEARSE & ENRICH

1. Encourage the ensemble members to each create their own ostinato – the motif can be taken directly from the song (complimentary ostinato) or created differently than the song (contrary ostinato).

2. Sing multiple melodic ostinati at the same time with the tune.

3. Melodic ostinati can be performed on pitched instruments to accompany the tune.

multiple melodic ostinati – *two or more melodic ostinatos performed simultaneously.*

Have a number of small groups of singers, each assigned a different melodic ostinato, perform at the same time while the rest of the ensemble sings the song.

ES/MS/HS: Rocky Mountain

Skin and Bones

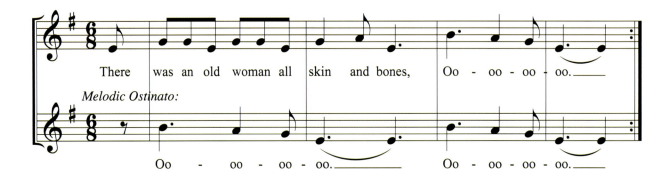

2. One night she thought she'd take a walk, oo-oo-oo-oo.

3. She walked by the old graveyard, oo-oo-oo-oo.

4. She saw the bones a lyin' a-round, oo-oo-oo-oo.

5. She went to the closet to get her broom, oo-oo-oo-oo.

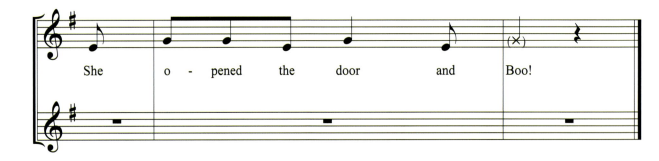

Rocky Mountain

2. Sunny valley, sunny valley, sunny valley low,
   When you're in that sunny valley, sing it soft and low. (Refrain)

3. Stormy ocean, stormy ocean, stormy ocean wide.
   When you're on that deep blue sea there's no place you can hide. (Refrain)

Rocky Mountain - *Ostinato*

Ostinato 1:
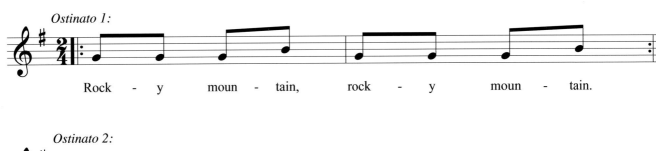

Ostinato 2:

Ostinato 3:

Ostinato 4:

Ostinato 5:
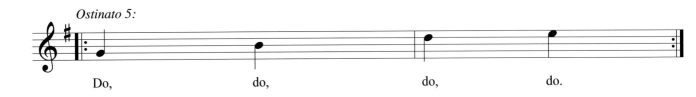

Ol' Joe Clark

Ol' Joe Clark

Verses

2. I went down to old Joe's house,
   Never been there before,
   He slept on the feather bed
   And I slept on the floor. (Refrain)

3. I went down to old Joe's house,
   He invited me to supper,
   I stumped my toe on the table leg
   And stuck my nose in the butter. (Refrain)

4. Old Joe Clark, he had a dog
   As blind as he could be;
   Chased a redbug 'round a stump
   And a coon up a hollow tree. (Refrain)

5. Old Joe Clark, he had a mule,
   His name was Morgan Brown,
   And every tooth in that mule's head
   Was sixteen inches around. (Refrain)

6. Joe Clark had a violin,
   Fiddled all the day,
   Let anybody start to dance
   And Joe would start to play. (Refrain)

CHAPTER 5

Teaching Procedures for
Part-Singing Skills in Polyphony

(Intersperse with Part-Singing Skills in Homophony)

canonic singing

combined canonic singing and ostinato

partner songs

layered song

canon

catch

descant

counter melody

two parts with self (polyphonic)

quodlibet

madrigal

multi-division polyphonic music

> **canonic singing** – songs which are not expressly composed as canons, but can be sung in imitation such as bitonic (sol-mi), tritonic (sol-mi-do), tetratonic (sol-mi-re-do), or pentatonic melodies (la-sol-mi-re-do).

Pedagogically referred to as *singing in canon*.

- **ES:** *Snail, Snail*
- **MS:** *The Birch Tree*
- **HS:** *Ol' Gray Goose*

SONG PREPARATION

1. Ensemble learns the song in the folk tradition.

FOUNDATION

1. Cruise control: if two cars are going the exact same speed but leave the starting line at different times, the car that left first will finish first, the car that left second will finish second.
2. While keeping a steady beat have the class chant 1, 2, 3, 4, 5, 6, 7, 8.
3. The class starts the chant again. The teacher can begin at any point later, but will not pass the first group, because everyone is counting at the same speed. Students start first and end first.

CORE KNOWLEDGE

1. Ensemble sings the melody (a.k.a. subject) with text with no teacher help.
2. Teacher instructs, "I'm going to do something different than you are doing; no matter what I sing you sing the song from the beginning to the end without stopping."
3. Ensemble sings the song and the teacher sings in canon by starting at the beginning of the song when the ensemble reaches number 2 in the music.
4. Teacher asks, "What did I do?" The class identifies that everyone sang the same song but the teacher started and ended at a different time than the class – just like counting to 8.
5. *Teacher:* "This as canonic singing because we are singing the same song but beginning at different times."
6. Practice again with the teacher singing second, then reverse and have the teacher begin first.

REHEARSE & ENRICH

1. The first practice after the CORE KNOWLEDGE lesson, divide the ensemble into two parts and have them sing in two part canon with no teacher help.

2. Sing numerous little tunes canonically.

3. Sing in canon in more than 2 parts.

Snail, Snail

The Birch Tree

Russian (in transliteration)

The Birch Tree
Verses

2. No one here would hurt you, O birch tree.
   Where is he who does not love the birch tree?Liuli, liuli O birch tree.
   Liuli, liuli O birch tree.

3. I will go alone to the forest,
   I will cut the birch in the forest,
   Liuli, liuli, the forest,
   Liuli, liuli, the forest.

4. O my little tree, I need three branches;
   For three silver pipes, I need three branches.
   Liuli, liuli, three branches,
   Liuli, liuli, three branches.

5. When I play my new balalaika,
   I will sing of you, my little birch tree.
   Liuli, liu, I'll be playing
   Liuli, liu, little birch tree.

2. Nyekomu byeryozu zalomati,
   Nyekomu kudryavu zashtshipati,
   Lyuli, lyuli, zalomati.
   Lyuli, lyuli, zalomati.

3. Paidu ya v lyes, pagulyayu,
   Byeluyu byeryozu zalomayu,
   Lyuli, lyuli, pagulyayu,
   Lyuli, lyuli, zalomayu.

4. Srezhu ya z byeryozyy tri prutotshka,
   Zdyelayu iz nyikh ya tri gudotshka,
   Lyuli, lyuli, tri prototshka,
   Lyuli, lyuli, tri gudotshka.

5. Tshetvertuya balalaiku,
   Staromu dyedu na zabavku,
   Lyuli, lyuli, balalaiku,
   Lyuli, lyuli, na zabavku.

Each successive voice part sings to the end of the song; there is no final chorded cadence.

This Russian text is transliterated (written in English sound-alike syllables rather than an actual language), so pronounce as written with both Liuli (English)/Lyuli (Russian transliteration) sounding as loo-lee [luli].

Ol' Gray Goose

2. She was climin' from the cart, Miss Susan lost her shoe;
   Stockin' had a big round hole, her foot was stickin' through. (Refrain)

> **combined canonic singing and ostinato** – *sing a song in canon while small groups of singers, each with a different melodic or rhythmic ostinato, perform at the same time.*

Previously learned songs in this sequence:

ES: *Bow Wow Wow* (canonic singing at one measure)
Skin and Bones (canonic singing at one measure)
Snail, Snail (canonic singing at two measures)

MS: *The Birch Tree* (canonic singing at one measure)
Great Big House (canonic singing at two measures)
Rocky Mountain (canonic singing at one measure)

HS: *Ah, Poor Bird* (canon at one measure)
Come, Let Us All A-Maying Go (canon at four measures)
Ol' Gray Goose (canon at one beat)
Sakura (canonic singing at two measures)

SONG PREPARATION

1. Ensemble has previously sung songs in canon and has sung songs accompanied with melodic or rhythmic ostinati.

FOUNDATION

1. Ensemble sings a song in canon, then they identify the skill as singing in canon.

2. Ensemble sings the same song with a melodic or rhythmic ostinato, then they identify the added part as a melodic or rhythmic ostinato.

CORE KNOWLEDGE

1. Ensemble sings the same song with ⅓ singers performing the melody, ⅓ singers performing in canon, and ⅓ singers performing with a melodic or rhythmic ostinato simultaneously.

2. Ensemble discusses the definition of singing in canon (canonic singing is singing the same song but different groups begin at different times) as well as the definition of melodic ostinato (a motif – short succession of notes – that is repeated at the same pitch throughout a piece of music) or rhythmic ostinato (rhythm pattern that is repeated throughout a piece of music).

REHEARSE & ENRICH

1. Sing in canon in multiple parts and add a number of melodic or rhythmic ostinati for an excellent practice of small groups holding their own part against others.

---

partner songs – *two songs which can be sung simultaneously because they have the same harmonic sequence or the same pentatonic properties; also called combinable songs.*

ES: *Don't Let the Wind* with *I Saw the Light*
MS: *Hurry, Hurry, Hurry* with *No Need to Hurry*
HS: *Go Down Moses* with *Joshua Fit the Battle of Jericho*
   Ensembles can sing the verses to *Go Down Moses* and add the partner song of *Joshua Fit the Battle of Jericho* with that refrain OR sing the verses to *Joshua Fit the Battle of Jericho* and add the partner song of *Go Down Moses* with that refrain.

SONG PREPARATION

1. Teach both songs in the folk tradition until the ensemble knows each tune well in unison singing.

FOUNDATION

1. Ensemble sings each song separately.

CORE KNOWLEDGE

1. Ensemble sings one song while the teacher sings the other at the same time.

2. Teacher asks, "What did I do while you sang your song?"; singers answer.

3. **Teacher:** "We are able to sing both of these songs at the same time because they are partner songs – they have the same harmonic properties."

4. Switch songs between teacher and ensemble then sing.

REHEARSE & ENRICH

1. ½ ensemble sings one song while ½ ensemble sings the other song; then switch songs.

2. Practice singing two very different songs at the same time (sounding badly) to show that songs are only partner songs if they have the same harmonic properties.

3. Older singers can identify the chords of the songs and discuss the meaning of the term harmonic properties (same chord progression).

Don't Let the Wind / I Saw the Light

Hurry, Hurry, Hurry / No Need to Hurry

Go Down Moses / Joshua Fit the Battle
Refrain

Go Down Moses
Verses

"Thus saith the Lord," bold Mos-es said, let my peo-ple go. "If

not, I'll smite your first-born dead," let my peo-ple go.

2. No more shall they in bondage toil, let my people go;
   Let them come out with Egypt's spoil, let my people go. (Refrain)

3. We need not always weep and mourn, let my people go;
   And wear those slavery chains forlorn, let my people go. (Refrain)

4. Come, Moses, you will not get lost, let my people go;
   Stretch out your rod and come across, let my people go. (Refrain)

5. As Israel stood by the water's side, let my people go;
   At God's command it did divide, let my people go. (Refrain)

6. When they had reached the other shore, let my people go;
   They sang a song of triumph o'er, let my people go. (Refrain)

7. O Moses, the cloud shall cleave the way, let my people go;
   A fire by night, a shade by day, let my people go. (Refrain)

8. Your foes shall not before you stand, let my people go;
   And you'll possess fair Canaan's land, let my people go. (Refrain)

9. This world's a wilderness of woe, let my people go;
   O let us on to Canaan go, let my people go. (Refrain)

10. O let us all from bondage flee, let my people go;
    And let us all in Christ be free, let my people go. (Refrain)

Joshua Fit the Battle
Verses

You may talk a-bout your king of Gid-e-on, You may talk a-bout your king of Saul; But there's none like good old Josh-u-a___ At the bat-tle of Jer-i-co.

2. Now the Lord commanded Joshua;
   "I command you and obey you must;
   You just march straight to those city walls
   And the walls will turn to dust." (Refrain)

3. Straight up to the walls of Jericho
   He marched with spear in hand,
   "Go blow that ram's horn," Joshua cried,
   "For the battle is in my hand." (Refrain)

4. The lamb ram sheep horns began to blow,
   And the trumpets began to sound,
   And Joshua commanded, "Now children, shout!"
   And the walls came tumbling down. (Refrain)

⎡ **layered song** – *a tune that is comprised of a number of phrases sung repeatedly, one on top of the other.*

ES: *Mofe Moni S'mo Hogbeke*
MS: *Banuwa Yo*
HS: *Lo Yisa Goy*

SONG PREPARATION

1. Teacher sings one musical phrase at a time and ensemble echoes each one.

FOUNDATION

1. Teacher leads ⅓ of the ensemble to sing and hold the note *"do."*

2. Teacher leads ⅓ of the ensemble to sing and hold the note *"mi"* on top of the *"do."*

3. Teacher leads ⅓ of the ensemble to sing and hold the note *"sol"* on top of the *"do"* and the *"mi."*

4. Continue singing in 3 parts using chords appropriate to the song being sung.

CORE KNOWLEDGE

1. Have different sections of the ensemble each sing one musical phrase so that all of the other sections listen to them.

2. Then, with only Layer 1 singing first, add each additional layer after the previous layer has successfully added their part, eventually working up to the entire piece.

3. *Teacher:* "Each section of the ensemble keeps singing the same musical phrase over and over, and because we start with Layer 1 and add on each additional phrase, this is called a layered song – we layer phrase on phrase like the layers of a cake from bottom to top."

REHEARSE & ENRICH

1. Some canons can be sung as layered songs.

2. Some layered songs can be sung as canons.

Mofe Moni S'mo Hogbeke
Yoruban

Can also be sung in the English adaption: Everybody loves Saturday night.

Banuwa Yo
Liberian

Lo Yisa Goy
Hebrew

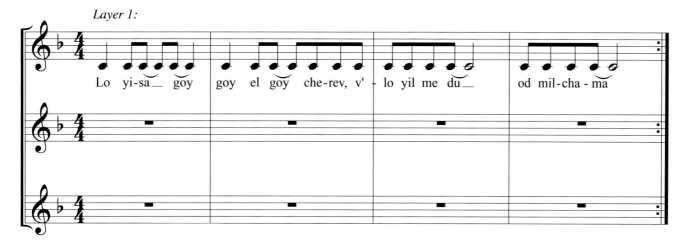
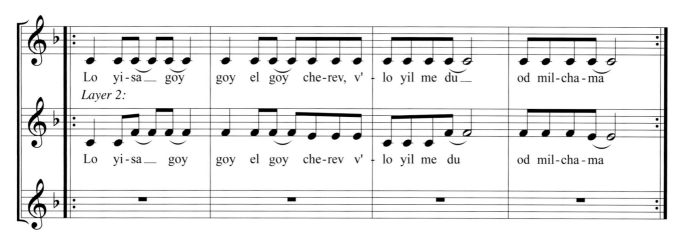
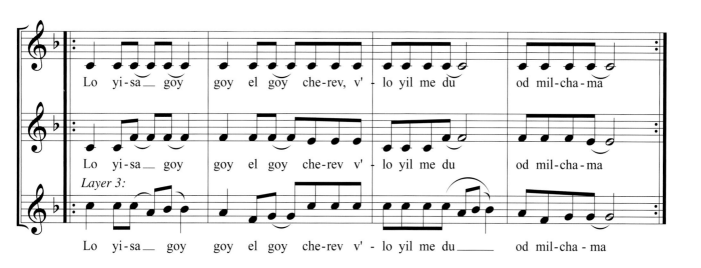

canon – *a melody [subject] sung by one voice part [dux] which is strictly imitated in another voice part [comes].*

Voice parts may enter at any interval of duration (canon of one measure, two measures), can be performed in augmentation (twice as slow) or in diminution (twice as fast), and can be sung at the unison or with different intervals between the voices (such as canon at the fifth), and can be performed in inversion, retrograde or retrograde inversion.

ES: *If You Dance*
MS: *Jesu, Meine Freude*
HS: *Non nobis, Domine*

SONG PREPARATION

1. The entire ensemble learns the melody [subject] of the canon through reading or by rote. It must be well known in unison before moving on.

FOUNDATION

1. Singers sing the song while the teacher claps the rhythm in canon.

CORE KNOWLEDGE

1. Ensemble sings the melody with text; teacher sings in canon.

2. Ensemble identifies that the teacher sang the same tune but began at a different time.

3. *Teacher:* "We are singing the same song but beginning at different times, however this song was specifically written to be sung this way and so we call this type of song a canon."

4. Practice again with the teacher singing second, then reverse and have the teacher begin first.

REHEARSE & ENRICH

1. Divide the ensemble into two parts and have them sing in canon with themselves.

2. Sing numerous canons in multiple parts.

3. When reading canons from notation, older singers should understand that the numbers indicate entrances and the cadence marks (🎵) indicate the held chord at the final cadence of the performance of the entire canon.

4. Teach older singers the musical terminology of *dux* and *comes* as well as figuring out a) interval of duration of entrances, b) augmentation or diminution, c) entrance at the unison or with different intervals between the voices, d) inversion, retrograde or retrograde inversion of the comes, etc.

If You Dance

▛ Cadence mark acts as a fermata only for the final cadence.

Jesu, Meine Fruede
German

Johann Crüger/Johann Franck

While both parts begin at the same time and have the same melody, Part 2 is in augmentation (twice as slow) as Part 1 and therefore follows behind in canon.

Non Nobis, Domine
Latin

William Byrd

One Accord • Developing Part-Singing Skills in School-Age Musicians

catch – *an English round of the 17th and 18th centuries, canonic in construction. Only when sung in parts would the words from one phrase 'catch' words in another phrase to create a sentence resulting in puns or double entendre.*

ES: *Sing Out*
  This catch results in the phrase: "sing out of tune."
MS: *There Once Was A Man from Calcutta*
  This catch results in the phrase: "ch-ch-ch-cheese, stutter, butter."
HS: *Catch 'round the Table (Now We Are Met)*
  This catch results in the phrase: "and let the catch and toast go 'round."

SONG PREPARATION

1. The ensemble must know how to sing in canon before singing a catch.

2. The entire ensemble learns the melody of the catch through reading or by rote. It must be well known in unison before moving on.

FOUNDATION

1. Number catch. Divide the class into three groups with each group clapping their own rhythm pattern individually, then together:

2. Teacher identifies that "while none of the three groups clap on all eight beats, when the three groups are combined there is clapping on all eight beats; the clapping from one part catches the clapping from the other parts so that all eight beats sound."

CORE KNOWLEDGE

1. Ensemble sings in 2 parts, then in 3 parts.

2. Teacher lets the singers comment on the text mingling within the multiple parts.

3. *Teacher:* "In this song, words from each phrase catch words in the other two phrases to make a complete sentence or idea. This is why this type of canon is called a catch."

REHEARSE & ENRICH

1. Have singers practice so that they don't punch out the words that catch each other but sing in a balanced way between all parts so that the text becomes obvious when sung.

2. Practice with other catches; these are especially fun for the audience in concerts.

Sing Out

There Once Was A Man from Calcutta

Catch 'round the Table
(Now We Are Met)

Samuel Webbe

◫ Cadence mark acts as a fermata only for the final cadence.

descant – *an independent melody that is often higher than and sometimes in contrary motion to the melody.*

- **ES:** *Suo Gan*
- **MS:** *Oleana*
- **HS:** *Wade in the Water*

SONG PREPARATION

1. Teach the descant first through reading or by rote.

FOUNDATION

1. As a warm-up, $2/3$ ensemble sings the well-known song *Hot Cross Buns* as $1/3$ ensemble sings the "sol" above the tonic note.
2. Singers derive the held note is higher.

CORE KNOWLEDGE

1. Ensemble sings the melody while the teacher sings the descant.
2. Singers must derive that their part is lower than the teacher's part.
3. *Teacher:* "A melody that accompanies the primary melody at higher pitches is called a descant."
4. Teacher sings the melody while the singers sing the descant.

REHEARSE & ENRICH

1. Ensemble can sing the melody while the descant is played on a cello, french horn, flute, recorder or other appropriate instrument for each song.
2. Older singers can sing tunes in multiple parts that also have descants.

Suo Gan
Welsh

Georgia Newlin, arr.

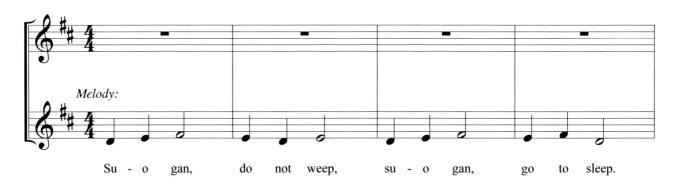

The Welsh pronunciation is see-oh gahn [sio gɑn].

Copyright © 2016 by MIE Publications

Oleana

Georgia Newlin, arr.

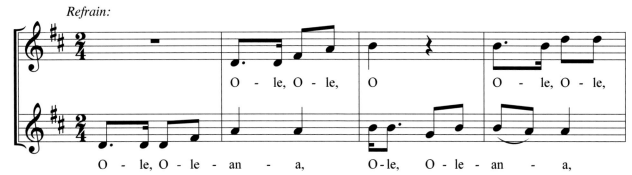

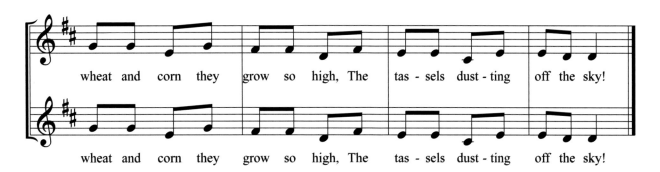

2. The hens lay eggs as big as rocks, Roosters crow like eight-day clocks;
Roasted pigs run all about with knives and forks stuck in their snouts! (Refrain)

Copyright © 2016 by MIE Publications

Oleana
Verses

3. The salmon leap so high up there, Hold your kettle in the air;
   They'll jump in, pull on the lid, And cook themselves to look like squid! (Refrain)

4. O come and bring your fiddle, Dance to the middle;
   Ole with his violin, Will help us make a merry din! (Refrain)

Wade in the Water

Georgia Newlin, arr.

Wade in the Water
Verses

2. Up on the mountain, Jehovah, He spoke, Wade in the water,
   Out of his mouth came fire and smoke, Wade in the water.

3. Down in the valley, down on my knees, Wade in the water,
   Asking my Lord to hear me, please, Wade in the water.

counter melody – *an independent melody that is subordinate to and often in contrary motion with the melody.*

ES: *Bye, Bye Baby*
MS: *The May Day Carol*
HS: *All the Pretty Little Horses*

SONG PREPARATION

1. Teach the counter melody first through reading or by rote.

FOUNDATION

1. As a warm-up, ensemble sings the well-known song, *Hot Cross Buns*.

2. ²/₃ ensemble sings *Hot Cross Buns* as ¹/₃ ensemble sings *do-re-mi-mi* [four times].

3. Singers derive the other melody [*do-re-mi-mi*] is generally in contrary motion (moves in opposite directions) much of the time.

CORE KNOWLEDGE

1. Ensemble sings the counter melody with no teacher assistance.

2. When the ensemble can sing the counter melody well, the teacher can sing the melody at the same time.

3. *Teacher:* "An independent melody that is subordinate to and often in contrary motion with the melody is called a counter melody."

REHEARSE & ENRICH

1. Ensemble reviews the counter melody.
2. Teach the melody through reading or by rote.
3. When well known, the ensemble sings the melody while the teacher sings the counter melody.
4. ½ ensemble sings melody while ½ ensemble sings counter melody; switch parts.
5. Eventually, have the ensemble identify and compare songs with descants [generally higher than the melody] and songs with counter melodies [generally in contrary motion to the melody].

Bye Bye Baby

Georgia Newlin, arr.

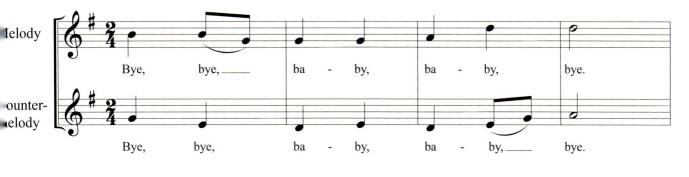

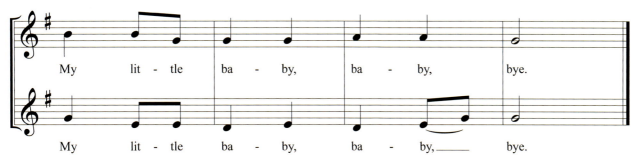

Copyright © 2016 by MIE Publications

The May Day Carol

Georgia Newlin, arr.

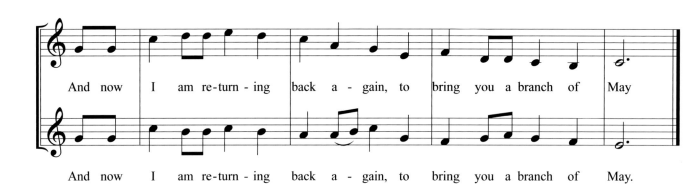

2. A branch of May, my dear, I say,
   Before your door I stand,
   It's nothing but a sprout, but it's well budded out,
   By the work of the Lord's own hand.

3. Go down in your dairy and fetch me a cup,
   A cup of your sweet cream,
   And, if I should live to tarry in the town,
   I will call on you next year.

4. When I am dead and in my grave,
   And covered with cold clay,
   The nightingale will sit and sing,
   And pass the time away.

5. In my pocket I've got a purse
   Tied up with a silken string,
   Nothing does it want but a little silver
   To line it well within.

6. My song is done, I must be gone,
   I can no longer stay,
   God bless you all both great and small,
   And send you a joyful May.

Copyright © 2016 by MIE Publications

All the Pretty Little Horses

Bethany Houff, arr.

Copyright © 2016 by MIE Publications

> **two parts with self (polyphonic)** – *one person simultaneously sings a song while performing a different rhythmic or melodic part through the use of body percussion, rhythm instruments, hand signs, or melodic instruments, etc.*

ES/MS/HS: *Lucy Locket / Hot Cross Buns*

Younger singers could

- sing a song while twirling around
- sing a song while playing a rhythmic ostinato on a percussion instrument
- sing a song while playing an easy melodic ostinato on a xylophone

To challenge advanced musicians, singers could

- sing a song while playing a melodic ostinato on a xylophone
- sing a canon or round while simultaneously performing the solfège of the melody in canon using hand signs or playing on a xylophone
- sing *Lucy Locket* while hand signing *Hot Cross Buns* and vice versa
- hand sign two songs at once while half of the ensemble sings the solfège of one song reading from the left hand signs and the other half of the ensemble sings the solfège of the other song reading from the right hand signs

You will want to begin this challenge for any grade-level of musician with elemental songs, and continue the activity over time progressing to actual two-part octavos using both polyphonic and homophonic pieces. This activity helps each section of the ensemble learn to hear the pitches of the other sections, which can lead to better intonation and deeper musical understanding of the pieces in the process.

Lucy Locket / Hot Cross Buns

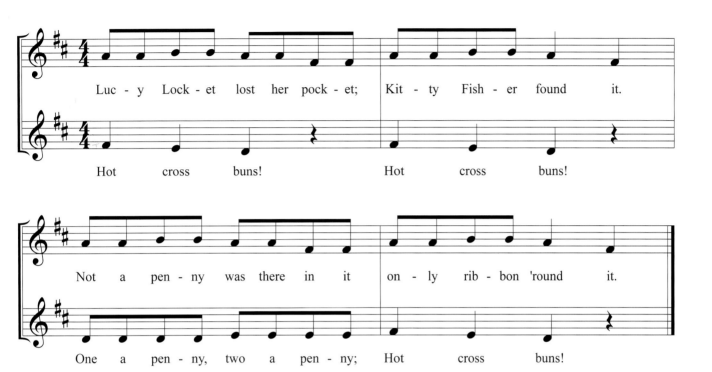

> **quodlibet** – *a collection of two or more tunes, often in no way related, which can be played or sung simultaneously because the progression of harmonic function is the same for each or mixed in some clever way, resulting in great fun or humor for the performer and audience.*

ES: Nursery Rhyme Quodlibet includes the tunes:
London Bridge is Falling Down
Mary Had A Little Lamb
Pease Porridge Hot

MS: *The Orchestra*

HS: Quodlibet in Nine Parts includes the tunes:
Coffee Canon
Music Alone Shall Live
The Shepherd

SONG PREPARATION

1. Over multiple class periods, ensemble learns each individual part or song of the quodlibet by reading or by rote.

FOUNDATION

1. Sing two well known partner songs at the same time.

CORE KNOWLEDGE

1. Divide the ensemble into multiple parts and have singers sing all of the parts of the quodlibet together at the same time.

2. *Teacher:* "The parts (each song or section) are put together to form a larger whole called a quodlibet that often produces fun and humor for the audience."

REHEARSE & ENRICH

1. Older singers can figure out other canons to sing as quodlibets with discussion of harmonic function (all songs sung together must have the same chord progression).

Nursery Rhyme Quodlibet

Ensemble can sing additional verses.

The Orchestra

English, German (see page 177)

Add one instrument at a time....

Quodlibet in Nine Parts:
Coffee Canon, Music Alone Shall Live, The Shepherd
English, German (see page 176)

Karl Gottlieb Hering

◨ Cadence mark acts as a fermata only for the final cadence.

[**madrigal** – *an unaccompanied polyphonic song for two or more voices with secular texts.*

ES: This music from the 15th-16th century was not composed for young children.
MS: *Fa La La*
HS: *Love Learns by Laughing*

FOUNDATION

1. Singers must have had lots of practice with easier polyphonic part-singing.

CORE KNOWLEDGE

1. Beginning with the bottom voice, have each section of the ensemble sing their part individually so that all of the other sections hear them.

2. Next, have two sections sing their parts at the same time eventually working up to the entire piece; always start with the bottom voice part first and add the next higher part.

REHEARSE & ENRICH

1. Sing other madrigals but be careful to study and understand the historical context of the text before giving them to school singers as many have hidden romantic subtexts.

2. Madrigals can be found at **cpdl.org**

Fa La La — Giovanni Maria Tasso

Fa La La *continued*

There were no words written with the original piece but was sung "fa, la, la" in the true madrigal style.

Love Learns by Laughing

Thomas Morley
Georgia Newlin, arr.

Copyright © 2016 by MIE Publications

Love Learns by Laughing *continued*

One Accord • Developing Part-Singing Skills in School-Age Musicians

Love Learns by Laughing *continued*

multi-division polyphonic music (polyphony) – *simultaneous individual voice parts with independent melodic movement.*

FOUNDATION

1. Ensemble sings previously learned canons, catches, glees, madrigals, partner songs, and quodlibets well.

CORE KNOWLEDGE

1. *Teacher:* "Each section of the ensemble is singing an individual part and each part has independent melodic movement – this is called polyphony."

2. Have singers identify songs and activities that are polyphonic such as canonic singing, combined canonic singing and ostinato, partner songs, layered songs, canons, catches, descants, counter melodies, two parts with self (polyphonic), quodlibets, madrigals, and other multi-division polyphonic music.

REHEARSE & ENRICH

1. Compare polyphony with homophony pointing out that polyphony is differing melodies/rhythms against each other (horizontal ideas) and homophony is generally homorhythmic and chordal (vertical ideas).

2. Have singers identify polyphonic and homophonic music as they are rehearsing their pieces throughout this sequence.

CHAPTER 6

Teaching Procedures for
Part-Singing Skills in Homophony
(Intersperse with Part-Singing Skills in Polyphony)

hand sign singing

interval singing

harmonic ending

round

chord root singing

vocal chording

parallel harmony

two parts with self (homophonic)

glee

chorale/hymn

multi-division homophonic music

hand sign singing – *singing in solfège from teacher's hand signs.*

Sequentially, this skill is taught first in unison, then in two parts that move at alternate times and, finally, in two parts that move simultaneously.

ES/MS/HS: *Scales*

SONG PREPARATION

1. Ensemble learns the solfège and hand signs for do pentatonic and la pentatonic scales.
2. Ensemble learns the solfège and hand signs for major and natural minor scales.
3. Ensemble sings scales from teacher's hand signs.

FOUNDATION

1. Sing in unison from teacher's hand signs.
2. Sing in two-parts from teacher's hand signs with each part moving at a different time.
3. Sing in two-parts from teacher's hand signs with both parts moving at the same time.
4. Two different singers can each lead a section of the ensemble for 2-part singing, three different singers can lead 3-part singing, etc.

CORE KNOWLEDGE

1. Ensemble can sing scales in parallel 3rds from teacher's hand signs.
2. Ensemble learns to sing and tune intervals from teacher's hand signs.
3. Ensemble can sing difficult passages from octavos from teacher's hand signs (without rhythmic context).

REHEARSE & ENRICH

1. Derive PREPARATION that come from the octavos you will be reading and singing during each rehearsal, for example:

    Sing the scale in the key signature of each piece of repertoire being sung during the rehearsal.

    Add the harmonic minor and melodic minor scales.

    Add modes.

2. Individual singers can each lead two sections of the ensemble for 4-part singing.

Scales

Do Pentatonic:

La Pentatonic:

Major:

Natural Minor:

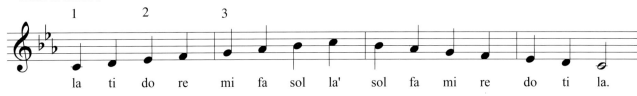

Scales can be sung in 2-part or 3-part canon by beginning at the entrance numbers 1, 2, and 3.

interval singing – *singers sing an interval with solfège and then with the interval name.*

This is not a theoretical lesson in major and minor; instead, it is the memorization of how a major triad feels/sounds versus how a minor triad feels/sounds. Music theory skills should be added to this type of exercise as singers progress through a K-12 choral program.

SONG PREPARATION

1. Ensemble sings solfège from teacher's hand signs in major and minor.

FOUNDATION

1. Teacher demonstrates *do-mi* interval while playing *do* on a keyboard and singing *mi* to create the sound of a major third.
2. Singers sing *do* while teacher sings *mi* and vice versa.
3. Teacher demonstrates *mi-sol* interval while playing *mi* on a keyboard and singing *sol* to create the sound of a minor third.
4. Singers sing *mi* while teacher sings *sol* and vice versa.

CORE KNOWLEDGE

1. Teacher sings, "*do – mi;* major third"; ensemble echoes.
2. Teacher sings, "*mi – sol*; minor third"; ensemble echoes.
3. Teacher sings, "*do – sol*; perfect fifth"; ensemble echoes.
4. Teacher sings, "*do – mi – sol*; major triad"; ensemble echoes.
5. **Teacher:** "The notes *do – mi – sol* make up the tonic triad in major. Knowing the size of the intervals (space between the notes) by ear helps tune those pitches."
6. Beginning on the same starting pitch, teacher sings "*la – do*; minor third"; ensemble echoes.
7. Teacher sings, "*do – mi;* major third"; ensemble echoes.
8. Teacher sings, "*la – mi;* perfect fifth"; ensemble echoes.
9. Teacher sings, "*la – do – mi*; minor triad"; ensemble echoes.
10. **Teacher:** "The notes *la – do – mi* make up the tonic triad in minor. Knowing the size of the intervals (space between the notes) by ear helps tune those pitches."

REHEARSE & ENRICH

1. Use the intervals to teach the singers to tune chords throughout the octavos the ensemble is rehearsing.

2. Be sure to practice chords found throughout the pieces, not just the tonic chord. The teacher should identify whether the chord is major or minor (or other): dominant chord, subdominant triad, dominant substitutions, all triads of the major and minor scales, secondary dominant chords, plus triads of the modes as needed.

harmonic ending – *adding a second part (or more) to the final note, notes, or phrase of a song, in order to harmonize a final tonic note as a chord.*

ES: *Liza Jane*
MS: *Bobo Leh Me 'Lone*
HS: *Ah! Vous Dirai Je, Maman*

SONG PREPARATION

1. Ensemble learns to sing a folksong with text from memory.

2. Singers can sing the folksong in solfège without any help from the teacher.

FOUNDATION

1. All singers sing *sol-fa-mi-re-do* down the scale.

2. Divide into groups. One group holds *sol* while the others descend, holding *do* to create the 5th interval.

3. A third group will sing *sol, fa,* then hold *mi* while the others repeat their pattern, creating a triad.

CORE KNOWLEDGE

1. Ensemble sings the folksong in solfège (using hand signs as appropriate) from memory or the board.

2. Teacher changes the last few notes of the tune on the board so that it ends on the fifth of the tonic chord; ensemble practices.

3. ½ the ensemble sings the song in solfège from the board with the fifth at the ending, ½ the ensemble sings the song in solfège with the original ending to produce harmony.

4. Teacher changes the last few notes of the tune on the board so that it ends on the third of the tonic chord; ensemble practices.

5. ½ the ensemble sings the song in solfège from the board with the third at the ending, ½ the ensemble sings the song in solfège with the original ending to produce harmony.

6. ⅓ the ensemble sings the third, ⅓ the ensemble sings the fifth, and ⅓ the ensemble sings the tonic (original ending) to produce a tonic chord at the end of the tune.

7. **Teacher:** "Since we are singing the last few words in multiple notes rather than as single notes, we are singing a harmonic ending because the notes produce harmony."

REHEARSE & ENRICH

1. Eventually, the ensemble can sing a chord at the end of each phrase (probably using mostly the dominant and tonic triads for folksongs).

Liza Jane

2. I've got a house in Baltimore, Li'l 'Liza Jane,
   Street car runs right by my door, Li'l 'Liza Jane.
   O, Eliza! Li'l 'Liza Jane.
   O, Eliza! Li'l 'Liza Jane.

3. I've got a house in Baltimore, Li'l 'Liza Jane,
   Brussels carpet on the floor, Li'l 'Liza Jane.
   O, Eliza! Li'l 'Liza Jane.
   O, Eliza! Li'l 'Liza Jane.

4. I've got a house in Baltimore, Li'l 'Liza Jane,
   Silver doorplate on the door, Li'l 'Liza Jane
   O, Eliza! Li'l 'Liza Jane.
   O, Eliza! Li'l 'Liza Jane.

Bobe Leh Me 'Lone

Bo - be, leh me 'lone, leh me 'lone, me no mar - ried yet, leh me 'lone.

When me mar - ried the bells go ring, when me mar - ried, conch shells go blow.

Bo - be, leh me 'lone, leh me 'lone, me no' mar - ried yet, leh me 'lone.

round – *a circular canon with several voices singing the same melody in overlapping succession, all entering on the same pitch as the first voice, returning to the beginning and singing (seemingly) without end. The melody consists of sections of equal length with the same underlying harmonic progression which, when sung together, produce harmony.*

ES: *Do, Re, Mi, Fa*
MS: *As I Mee Walkéd*
HS: *Fanny*

SONG PREPARATION

1. The entire ensemble learns the melody of the round through reading or by rote. It must be well known in unison before moving on.

FOUNDATION

1. Singers sing the song while the teacher claps the rhythm as a round.

CORE KNOWLEDGE

1. Ensemble sings the subject on text; teacher sings the same tune but enters later.
2. Ensemble identifies that the teacher sang the same tune but began at a different time.
3. Ensemble identifies this as canon – singing the same song but beginning at different times.
4. *Teacher:* "This is a special type of canon – called a round - because the end of the song forces you to return to the beginning like a circle (i.e. you have to go around)."

REHEARSE & ENRICH

1. The first practice, divide the ensemble into two or three parts and have them sing the round by themselves.
2. Sing numerous rounds in multiple parts; compare canons with rounds.
3. When reading rounds from notation, older singers should understand that the numbers indicate entrances and the cadence marks (𝄐) indicate the held chord at the final cadence of the performance of the entire canon.

Do Re Mi Fa

The School Round Book, 1852

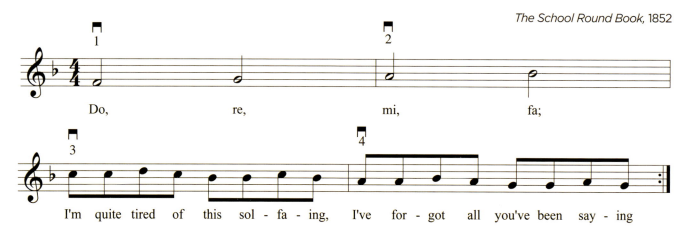

◻ Cadence mark acts as a fermata only for the final cadence.

As I Mee Walkéd

Pammelia by Thomas Ravenscroft

Each successive voice part finishes with "cuckoo"; there is no final chorded cadence.

Fanny

Anonymous, ca 1769

◼ Cadence mark acts as a fermata only for the final cadence.

chord root singing – one group sings the melody of a song while another group sings the chord roots; also referred to as bass line singing or root melody.

- **ES:** *Skip to My Lou*
- **MS:** *Sandy Land*
- **HS:** *Down in the Valley*

SONG PREPARATION

1. Teach the song in the folk tradition over a number of class periods until the ensemble knows the tune well in unison singing.

FOUNDATION

1. Teacher leads singers with the following echo patterns:

    do-mi-sol-mi-do

    sol,-ti,-re-ti,-sol,

CORE KNOWLEDGE

1. When the ensemble can sing the song without help from the teacher, the teacher can sing a bass line (made up of the roots of the accompanying chords) using the notes *do* for the tonic function and *low sol* for the dominant functions.
2. Ensemble identifies that the teacher sang *do* and *low sol.*
3. Ensemble sings the bass line from the teacher's hand signs.
4. Ensemble sings the bass line from the teacher's hand signs while the teacher sings the melody.
5. ½ the ensemble sings the melody and ½ the ensemble sings the bass line.
6. *Teacher:* "We are singing the melody and the bass line which is also known as chord root singing."

REHEARSE & ENRICH

1. Practice with other songs that use the tonic and dominant function, permitting the singers to figure out the bass line.
2. As the ensemble learns more about triads help singers understand that the term root of the chord means the lowest note of each chord in root position.
3. Add tunes that include the subdominant function (*fa*).
4. Be sure to sing tunes in minor or modes.
5. Eventually sing tunes that include other chords such as supertonic (ii = *re*), mediant (iii = *mi*), submediant (vi = *la*), and leading tone (vii° = *ti*) in major; supertonic (ii° = *ti*), mediant (III = *do*), submediant (VI = *fa*), and leading tone (vii° = *si*) in harmonic minor.

Skip to My Lou

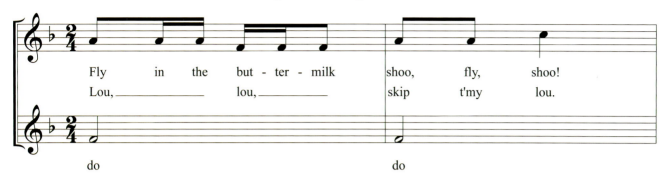

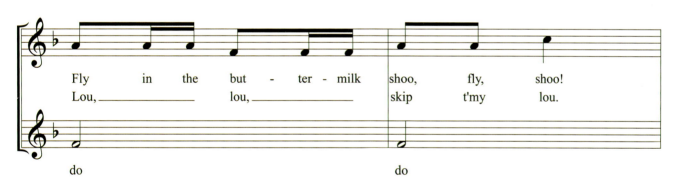
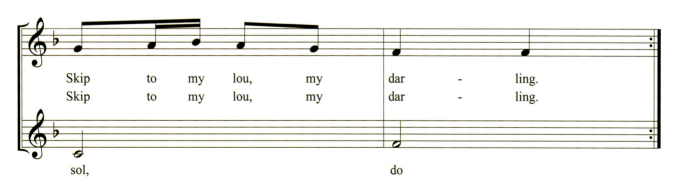

2. Lost my partner, what'll I do? (Refrain)
3. I'll get another, handsomer than you! (Refrain)
4. Little red wagon, painted blue! (Refrain)

Sandy Land

2. Hoeing taters in Sandy land (3x); Fare thee well, good ladies.
3. No more hoeing in Sandy land (3x); Fare thee well, good ladies.
4. One more river I'm bound to cross (3x); 'Till I meet my honey.
5. Hop come along, my pretty little miss (3x); Marry you next Sunday.

Down in the Valley

Verses

3. Throw your arms 'round me before it's too late,
   Throw your arms 'round me, feel my heart break.
   Feel my heart break, dear, feel my heart break,
   Throw your arms 'round me, feel my heart break.

4. If you don't love me, none else will do,
   My heart is breaking, dear, just for you.
   Breaking for you, dear, breaking for you,
   My heart is breaking, dear, just for you.

5. Writing this letter, containing three lines,
   Answer my question: Will you be mine?
   Will you be mine, dear, will you be mine?
   Answer my question: Will you be mine?

6. Build me a castle forty feet high,
   So's I can see him as he goes by,
   As he goes by, dear, as he goes by,
   So's I can see him as he goes by.

7. Down in the valley, the mocking bird wings,
   Telling my story, here's what he sings:
   Roses love sunshine, violets love dew,
   Angels in heaven knows I love you.

8. Knows I love you, dear, knows I love you,
   Angels in heaven knows I love you.
   Knows I love you, dear, knows I love you,
   Angels in heaven knows I love you.

vocal chording – *one group sings the melody while two or more other groups sing the chord tones; chord inversions are often used so that the movement between the tones in each voice part is minimal.*

- **ES:** *Aunt Rhody*
- **MS:** *Joe Turner Blues*
- **HS:** *The Lion Sleeps Tonight*

SONG PREPARATION

1. Teach the song in the folk tradition over a number of class periods until the ensemble knows and performs the tune well in unison.

FOUNDATION

1. Teacher plays two pitches of the triads from the chord progression below (bold notes are the roots of the chords and can be gently stressed above the others). Singers sing the third pitch to build aural awareness. Repeat by switching parts.

sol	**sol**	sol
mi	fa	mi
do	ti,	**do**
I	V7	I

CORE KNOWLEDGE

1. When the ensemble can sing the song without help from the teacher, the teacher identifies the notes *do-mi-sol* as the tonic triad and identifies the notes *ti,-fa-sol* as the (incomplete) dominant seventh triad.

2. Teacher divides ensemble into three parts and assigns each part to one note from the tonic triad and one note from the dominant triad (reading straight across the written row).

3. Teacher holds up one finger and the ensemble sings the tonic triad, teacher holds up five fingers and the ensemble sings the dominant triad; practice until the ensemble can move smoothly between the chords.

4. Teacher sings the song while holding up one or five fingers so that the students sing the correct chords to accompany the song.

5. *Teacher:* "This singing skill is vocal chording because you're singing chords along with the melody."

6. As needed: teacher identifies the subdominant chord as *fa,-la,-do*.

7. Teacher holds up four fingers and the ensemble sing the subdominant chord; practice until the ensemble can move smoothly between the three chords.

sol	*la*	*sol*	***sol***	*sol*
mi	***fa***	*mi*	*fa*	*mi*
do	*do*	***do***	*ti,*	***do***
I	IV	I	V7	I

REHEARSE & ENRICH

1. First, practice by holding out the chords with solos or small groups singing the melody.

2. Second, the ensemble can sing the text to the song while singing their pitches of the chords (rather than just holding out the notes in solfège).

3. SATB/SSAA/TTBB ensembles can sing the seventh chords with all four notes.

Aunt Rhody

Georgia Newlin, arr.

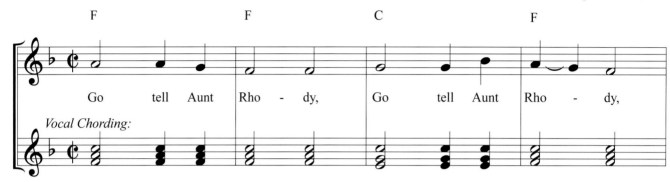

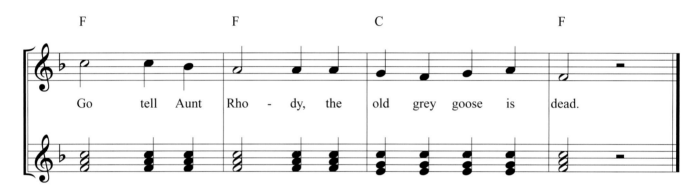

2. The one she's been saving,
   The one she's been saving,
   The one she's been saving,
   To make a feather bed.

3. The old grander's weeping,
   The old grander's weeping,
   The old grander's weeping,
   Because his wife is dead.

4. The goslings are mourning,
   The goslings are mourning,
   The goslings are mourning,
   Because their mother's dead.

5. She died in the millpond,
   She died in the millpond,
   She died in the millpond,
   Standing on her head.

Copyright © 2016 by MIE Publications

Joe Turner Blues

Georgia Newlin, arr.

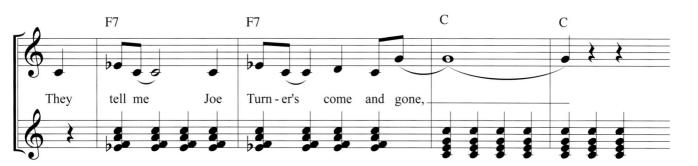

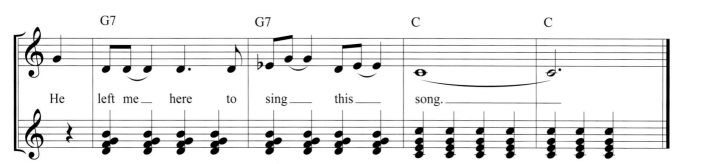

2. He came here with forty links of chain.
   He came here with forty links of chain.
   He left me here to sing this song.

3. Joe Turner, he took my man away.
   Joe Turner, he took my man away.
   He left me here to sing this song.

Copyright © 2016 by MIE Publications

The Lion Sleeps Tonight

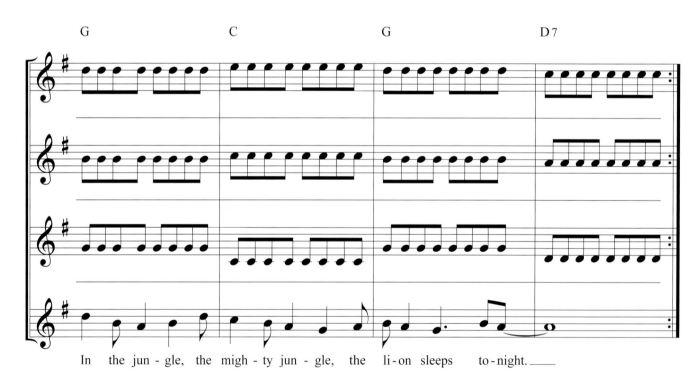

parallel harmony – *adding a line with consistently parallel third intervals or parallel sixth intervals to the melody. Generally, when the melody begins on the tonic (Alouette) or third (El Flórón), the harmony is sung a third above or a sixth below; when the melody begins on the fifth (De Colores), the harmony is sung a third below or a sixth above.*

ES: *Alouette*
MS: *El Flóron*
HS: *De Colores*

SONG PREPARATION

1. Teach the song in the folk tradition over a number of class periods until the ensemble knows the tune well in unison singing.

FOUNDATION

1. ½ ensemble sings the major scale (E♭M) at the same time ½ ensemble sings the natural minor scale (Cm) both ascending and descending.

2. Switch parts.

CORE KNOWLEDGE

1. Ensemble sings the song very softly while the teacher sings the parallel harmony.

2. Teacher asks the ensemble to explain what they heard.

3. *Teacher:* "I sang parallel harmony with your melody. When the melody begins on the tonic or third, the harmony is sung a third above or a sixth below; when the melody begins on the fifth, the harmony is sung a third below or a sixth above."

REHEARSE & ENRICH

1. Continue to sing songs with parallel harmony, eventually having the ensemble improvise their own.

2. Parallel harmony can be played on recorder, flutes or other instruments appropriate to each particular song.

Alouette

French

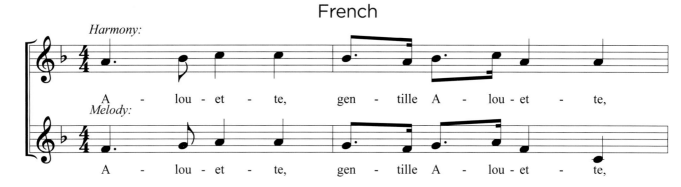

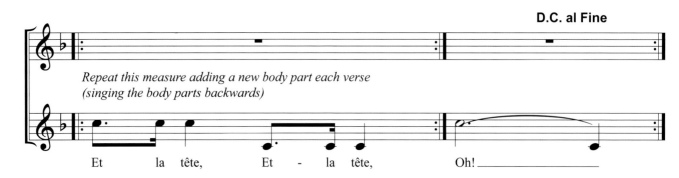

1. Et la bec, (the beak)   3. Et le cou, (the neck)   4. Et le dos, (the back)   5. Et les pattes, (the feet)

El Florón
Spanish

El Florón

GAME DIRECTIONS

Group stands in a circle and passes a ball while singing. The one with the ball in hand on the first beat of the last measure is out and must sit in place.

For older students, pass multiple balls at once. Those seated may try to knock the ball out of play but must not let their bottoms leave the ground while doing so.

De Colores

Spanish

De Colores *continued*

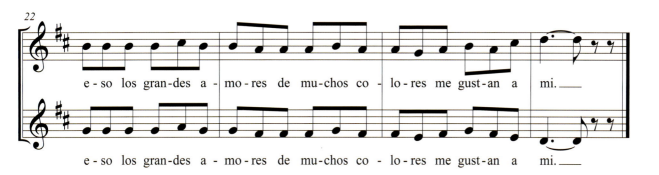

two parts with self (homophonic) – *one person simultaneously sings a song while performing a homorhythmic harmonic part through the use of body percussion, rhythm instruments, hand signs, or melodic instruments, etc.*

While using homophonic music previously learned in this sequence, younger singers could

- sing a song while clapping the rhythm of the song
- sing a song while playing the chord roots on a barred percussion instrument

To challenge advanced musicians, singers could

- sing a song while using hand signs to show the chord roots
- accompany their own singing with chorded zither, lap dulcimer, guitar or ukulele

You will want to begin this challenge for any grade-level of musician with elemental songs, and continue the activity over time progressing to actual two-part octavos using both polyphonic and homophonic pieces. This activity helps each section of the ensemble learn to hear the other parts of the song, which can lead to better intonation and deeper musical understanding of the pieces in the process.

> **glee** – *an 18th century genre of unaccompanied English choral music in three or more parts for solo men's voices (including male alto); generally brief, constructed in sections, and homophonic. Some glees can be sung by either treble or mixed voices.*

ES: These 18th century songs were not composed for young children.
MS: *Si Cantare*
HS: *Let Mirth and Joy A-bound*

FOUNDATION

1. Ensemble learns the song or the parts separately through reading or by rote.

CORE KNOWLEDGE

1. Ensemble sings through the melody in unison.

2. Ensemble sings in 2-parts.

3. Ensemble sings in 3-parts.

4. Teacher gives the definition of a glee and identifies that the class is currently singing a glee; singers give reasons why it is a glee.

REHEARSE & ENRICH

1. Many glees were of a comical or bawdy nature – have singers describe the mood of the particular glee they are singing.

2. Have sections sing different parts of the glee to see how the words fit together.

Si Cantare

Italian

Antonio Caldara

◨ Cadence mark acts as a fermata only for the final cadence.

Let Mirth And Joy Abound

Thomas Linley the elder

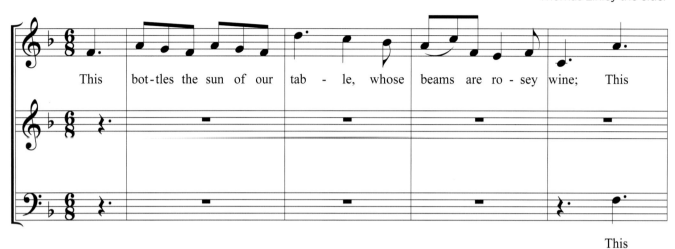
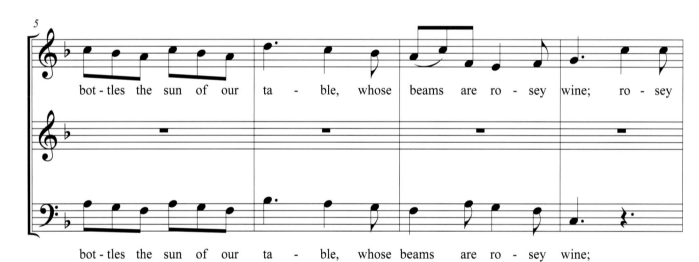
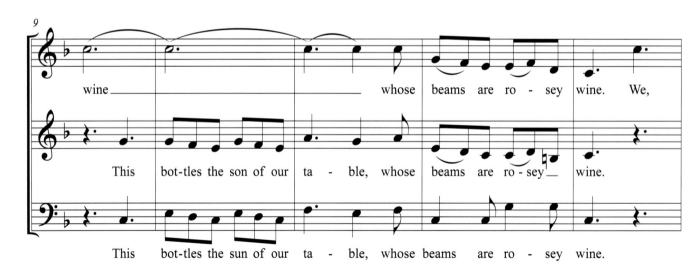

Let Mirth And Joy Abound *continued*

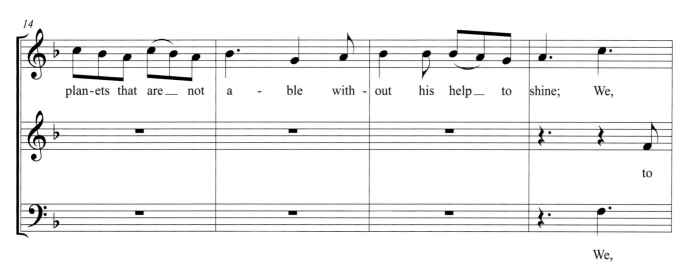

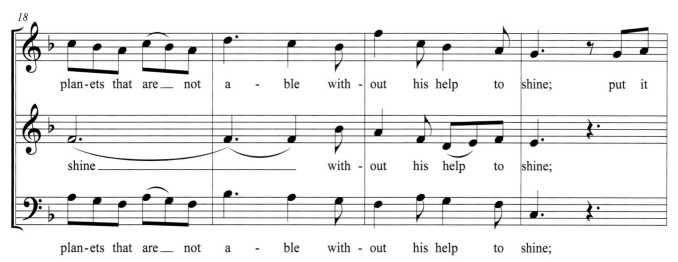

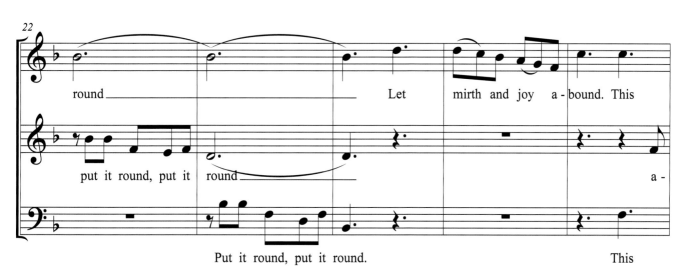

Let Mirth And Joy Abound *continued*

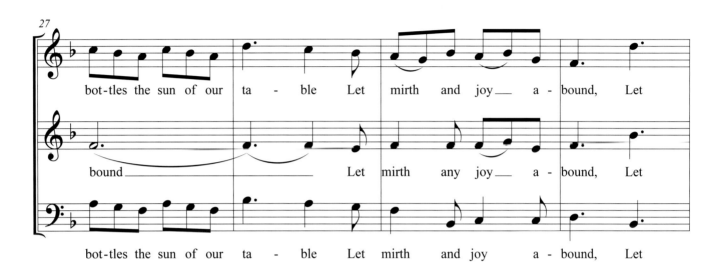
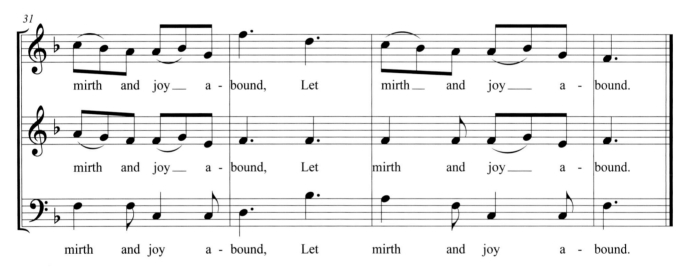

chorale / hymn – *Protestant metrical hymn tune originally sung in unison that was then harmonized in multiple-part settings during the 16th-17th centuries. These harmonized melodies are also referred to as hymns.*

ES: The harmonizations of these chorale tunes were not composed for young children.
MS: *O Sacred Head* – chorale melody
　　Singers sing the melody while teacher plays the 4-part chorale on the piano or have the singers sing along with a recording in order to introduce the concept of harmonized parts.
HS: *O Sacred Head* – chorale

SONG PREPARATION

1. Ensemble listens to a recording of a chorale and tries to pick out the melody by ear.
2. Ensemble learns chorale melody by reading or from teacher's hand signs.

FOUNDATION

1. Ensemble reads bass part in solfège.
2. Ensemble reads tenor part in solfège.
3. Ensemble reads alto part in solfège.

CORE KNOWLEDGE

1. Singers compare the rhythm of the three parts with the melody.
2. *Teacher:* "Most of the rhythms of all three parts are the same due to the text."
3. Teacher defines chorale and identifies this melody as a chorale tune.
4. Sing various chorale tunes using solfège.
5. Sing chorales in 2- and 3-parts.

REHEARSE & ENRICH

1. Ensemble sings the bass and middle parts together.
2. Ensemble sings the bass and melody parts together.
3. Ensemble sings the middle and melody parts together.
4. Ensemble sings all four parts together.
5. Review 'chorale' definition by having the singers identify the features of a chorale: melody is an old tune, harmonized in parts, generally uses homorhythmic texture.

O Sacred Head

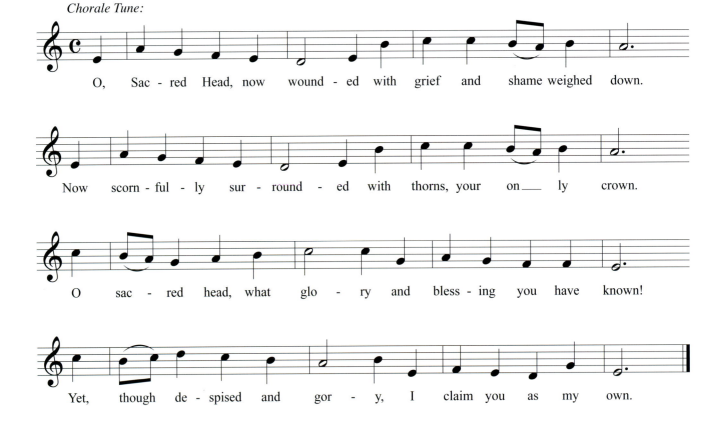

O Sacred Head, Now Wounded

Hans Leo Hassler

multi-division homophonic music (homophony) – *the combination of voice parts of similar rhythmic design with the melody concentrated in one voice part such as melody-plus-accompaniment (singing a song with guitar), or homorhythmic (rhythms are the same or similar among all of the parts) textures found in hymns and chorales.*

ES: *Skip to My Lou*
     Teacher accompanies with an instrument such as guitar or banjo.
MS: *Aro Que Nostre Seigne Es Nat*
HS: *Maoz Tsur*

SONG PREPARATION

1. Ensemble learns and sings the tune to the song in unison.

FOUNDATION

1. Ensemble sings the tune in unison while the teacher accompanies them with piano, guitar, or autoharp, etc.

CORE KNOWLEDGE

1. Elementary singers produce harmony by singing the melody while the teacher plays an homorhythmic accompaniment on an instrument. Older singers produce their own homophony by singing in 2-, 3-, or more parts.

2. *Teacher:* "Homophony is generally homorhythmic (rhythms are the same or very similar among all of the parts)."

3. Have singers identify songs and activities that are homophonic such as hand sign singing, interval singing, harmonic endings, rounds, chord root singing, vocal chording, parallel harmony, two parts with self, glees, chorales/hymns, and another multi-division homophonic music.

REHEARSE & ENRICH

1. Compare homophony with polyphony. Point out that homophony is homorhythmic (generally, all parts have the same rhythm at the same time) and chordal (vertical ideas). Point out that polyphony is characterized by independent melodies against each other (horizontal ideas).

Skip to My Lou

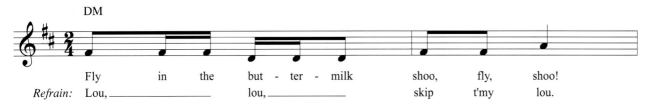
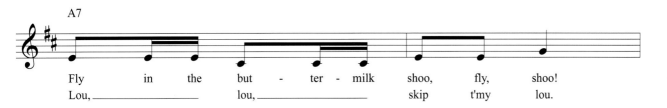

2. Lost my partner, what'll I do? (Refrain)

3. I'll get another, handsomer than you! (Refrain)

4. Little red wagon, painted blue! (Refrain)

Aro Que Nostre Seigne Es Nat

Provençal (French)

15c Provençal Carole

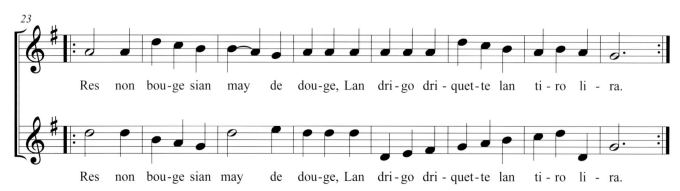

Maoz Tsur

Hebrew

Georgia Newlin, arr.

Copyright © 2016 by MIE Publications

Alphabetical Song List

Song Title	Source	Page
Ah, Poor Bird	*The Temple Choir* songbook, 1871	64, 172
Ah! Vous Dirai Je, Maman	France	124, 172
Alouette	French Canadian	138, 172
All the Pretty Little Horses	United States – Black tradition	103
Aro Que Nostre Seigne Es Nat	15c Provençal Carole	152, 173
As I Mee Walkéd	*Pammelia* (Ravenscroft)	126
Aunt Rhody	United States	134
Banuwa Yo	Liberia	86, 173
Birch Tree, The	Russia	73, 173
Bobo Leh Me 'Lone	Trinidad & Tobago	123
Bow Wow Wow	United States	62
Buffalo Boy	United States – West Virginia	26
Bye, Bye Baby	United States – Appalachia	101
Catch 'round the Table	Samuel Webbe	94
Chantey	Sea Chantey	41
Coffee Canon from "Quodlibet in Nine Parts"	Karl Gottlieb Hering	109, 176
Come, Let Us All A-Maying Go	John Hilton	40
Dance Josey	United States Play Party – Texas	30
De Colores	United States – Texas, New Mexico	140, 175
Devil's Nine Questions, The	United States – Virginia, Kentucky	60
Do, Re, Mi, Fa	*The School Round Book*, 1852	126
Don't Let the Wind	United States – St. Helena Island, NC	79
Down in the Valley	United States – Kentucky	131
El Flóron	Puerto Rico	139, 175
Fa La La	Giovanni Maria Tasso	110
Fanny	Anonymous, ca 1769	127
Farmer in the Dell, The	England, United States, Canada	28
Father Grumble	United States – New England	17
Go Down, Moses	United States – Spiritual	81, 82
God Bless the Moon	United States – Kentucky	51
Great Big House	United States Play Party	63
Hill and Gully Rider	Jamaica	39
Hot Cross Buns	United States	105
Hurry, Hurry, Hurry	Calypso style	80
I Saw the Light	White Southern Spiritual	79
If You Dance	Hungary	89
Jesu, Meine Freude	J. Crüger / J. Franck	90, 175
Joe Turner Blues	United States – Blues	135
John the Rabbit	United States – Black tradition	57
Johnny On a Woodpile	United States	20
Joshua Fit the Battle of Jericho	United States – Spiritual	81, 83
Lavender's Blue	England	50

Song Title	Source	Page
Let Mirth and Joy A-bound	Thomas Linley the elder	144
Lion Sleeps Tonight, The	South Africa	136
Liza Jane	United States – Maryland	122
Lo Yisa Goy	Israel	87, 175
London Bridge is Falling Down from "Nursery Rhyme Quodlibet"	England	107
Love Learns by Laughing	Thomas Morley	112
Lucy Locket	British Isles, United States	105
Maoz Tsur	Israel – Hanukkah	153, 176
Mary Had A Little Lamb from "Nursery Rhyme Quodlibet"	England	107
May Day Carol, The	England – May Day carol	102
Mofe Moni S'mo Hogbeke	Nigeria	85, 176
Music Alone Shall Live from "Quodlibet in Nine Parts"	Karl Gottlieb Hering	109, 177
My Good Old Man	United States	25
No Need to Hurry	Calypso style	80
Non nobis, Domine	William Byrd	91, 177
O Sacred Head	Hans Leo Hassler	148, 149
Ol' Gray Goose	United States	75
Ol' Joe Clark	United States – Tennessee, Texas	69
Ol' Texas	United States – Cowboy Song	22
Oleana	United States – Minnesota	97
Orchestra, The	Germany	108, 177
Pease Porridge Hot from "Nursery Rhyme Quodlibet"	England	107
Rocky Mountain	United States	67
Sail Away Ladies	United States – Tennessee	59
Sakura	Japan	55, 178
Sandy Land	United States – North Carolina	130
Sea Shell	United States – New England	53
Shepherd, The from "Quodlibet in Nine Parts"	Karl Gottlieb Hering	109, 177
Si Cantare	Antonio Caldara	143, 177
Sing Out	England	93
Skin and Bones	United States – Kentucky, Tennessee	66
Skip to My Lou	United States – Tennessee	129, 151
Snail, Snail	United States – Mississippi	73
Suo Gan	Wales	96
Sweet William	United States – Southern Appalachia	18
There Once Was A Man from Calcutta	United States – New England	93
There's A Hole in the Bucket	United States – Pennsylvania German	24
Tom Dooley	United States – North Carolina	54
Tongo	Polynesian Islands	21, 178
Turn the Glasses Over	United States – Ohio, Virginia	32
Twinkle Little Star	"The Star" by J. Taylor (1806)/France	16, 43, 45, 46
Wade in the Water	United States – Spiritual	99
Who's That?	England, United States – Appalachia	49

Elementary School Song List (suggested)

Song Title	Page
Alouette	138, 172
Aunt Rhody	134
Bow Wow Wow	62
Bye, Bye Baby	101
Do, Re, Mi, Fa	126
Don't Let the Wind	79
Farmer in the Dell, The	28
Hill and Gully Rider	59
Hot Cross Buns	105
I Saw the Light	79
If You Dance	89
John the Rabbit	57
Johnny On a Woodpile	20
Liza Jane	122
London Bridge is Falling Down from "Nursery Rhyme Quodlibet"	107
Lucy Locket	105
Mary Had A Little Lamb from "Nursery Rhyme Quodlibet"	107
Mofe Moni S'mo Hogbeke	85, 176
Sea Shell	53
Sing Out	93
Skin and Bones	66
Skip to My Lou	129, 151
Snail, Snail	73
Suo Gan	96
There's A Hole in the Bucket	24
Twinkle Little Star	16, 43, 45, 46
Who's That?	49

Middle School Song List (suggested)

Song Title	Page
Aro Que Nostre Seigne Es Nat	152, 173
As I Mee Walkéd	126
Banuwa Yo	86, 173
Birch Tree, The	73, 173
Bobo Leh Me 'Lone	123
Come, Let Us All A-Maying Go	40
Dance Josey	30
El Flóron	139, 175
Fa La La	110
Father Grumble	17
Great Big House	63
Hot Cross Buns	105
Hurry, Hurry, Hurry	80
Jesu, Meine Freude	90, 175
Joe Turner Blues	135
Lavender's Blue	50
Lucy Locket	105
May Day Carol, The	102
My Good Old Man	25
No Need to Hurry	80
O Sacred Head	148
Oleana	97
Orchestra, The	108, 177
Rocky Mountain	67
Sail Away Ladies	59
Sandy Land	130
Si Cantare	143, 177
There Once Was A Man from Calcutta	93
Tom Dooley	54
Tongo	21, 178
Twinkle Little Star	16, 43, 45, 46

One Accord • Developing Part-Singing Skills in School-Age Musicians

High School Song List (suggested)

Song Title	Page
Ah, Poor Bird	64, 172
Ah! Vous Dirai Je, Maman	124, 172
All the Pretty Little Horses	103
Buffalo Boy	26
Catch 'round the Table	94
Chantey	41
Coffee Canon from "Quodlibet in Nine Parts"	109, 176
De Colores	140, 175
Devil's Nine Questions, The	60
Down in the Valley	131
Fanny	127
Go Down, Moses	81, 82
God Bless the Moon	51
Hot Cross Buns	105
Joshua Fit the Battle of Jericho	81, 83
Let Mirth and Joy A-bound	144
Lion Sleeps Tonight, The	136
Lo Yisa Goy	87, 175
Love Learns by Laughing	112
Lucy Locket	105
Maoz Tsur	153, 176
Music Alone Shall Live from "Quodlibet in Nine Parts"	109, 176
Non nobis, Domine	91, 177
O Sacred Head	149
Ol' Gray Goose	75
Ol' Joe Clark	69
Ol' Texas	22
Sakura	55, 178
Shepherd, The from "Quodlibet in Nine Parts"	109, 177
Sweet William	18
Turn the Glasses Over	32
Twinkle Little Star	16, 43, 45, 46
Wade in the Water	99

Three Note Melodies (Tritonic)

Song Title	Scale / Mode	Page
Hot Cross Buns	do tritonic	105
Lucy Locket	mi tritonic	105
Snail, Snail	mi tritonic	73
Suo Gan	do tritonic	96

Do-centered Melodies

Song Title	Scale / Mode	Page
Ah! Vous Dirai Je, Maman	do hexachord	124, 172
Alouette	do hexachord	138, 172
As I Mee Walkéd	Ionian	126
Aunt Rhody	do pentachord	134
Banuwa Yo	do hexachord	83, 173
Bobo Leh Me 'Lone	diatonic major w/fi	123
Bow Wow Wow	do pentatonic	62
Buffalo Boy	do tetratonic	26
Bye, Bye Baby	do tetratonic melody	101
Catch 'round the Table	diatonic major	94
Coffee Canon from "Quodlibet in Nine Parts"	do hexachord	109, 176
Come, Let Us All A-Maying Go	diatonic major	40
Dance Josey	do pentatonic – extended	30
De Colores	diatonic major w/ta	140, 175
Devil's Nine Questions, The	do pentatonic – extended	60
Do, Re, Mi, Fa	do hexachord	126
Don't Let the Wind	do pentatonic – extended	79
Down in the Valley	do hexachord	131
El Flóron	diatonic major	139, 175
Fanny	diatonic major w/fi	127
Farmer in the Dell, The	do pentatonic – extended	28
Father Grumble	do pentatonic – extended	17
Great Big House	do pentatonic	63
Hill and Gully Rider	do pentatonic – extended	39
Hot Cross Buns	do tritonic	105
Hurry, Hurry, Hurry	do hexachord	80
I Saw the Light	do pentatonic – extended	79
Johnny On a Woodpile	do pentachord – extended	20

One Accord • Developing Part-Singing Skills in School-Age Musicians

Do-centered Melodies (continued)

Song Title	Scale/Mode	Page
Lavender's Blue	Ionian	50
Let Mirth and Joy A-bound	diatonic major	144
Lion Sleeps Tonight, The	do pentachord melody	136
Liza Jane	do pentatonic – extended	122
London Bridge is Falling Down from "Nursery Rhyme Quodlibet"	do hexachord	107
Love Learns by Laughing	Ionian w/fi, si, di	112
Maoz Tsur	Ionian melody	153, 176
Mary Had A Little Lamb from "Nursery Rhyme Quodlibet"	do tetratonic	107
May Day Carol, The	diatonic major	102
Mofe Moni S'mo Hogbeke	diatonic major	85, 176
Music Alone Shall Live from "Quodlibet in Nine Parts"	diatonic major	109, 176
No Need to Hurry	diatonic major	80
Non nobis, Domine	Mixolydian	91, 177
Ol' Texas	do pentatonic – extended	22
Oleana	diatonic major	97
Orchestra, The	diatonic major	108, 177
Pease Porridge Hot from "Nursery Rhyme Quodlibet"	do tetrachord	107
Rocky Mountain	do pentatonic	67
Sail Away Ladies	do pentatonic – extended	59
Sandy Land	do hexachord	130
Sea Shell	do tetratonic	53
Shepherd, The from "Quodlibet in Nine Parts"	diatonic major	109, 177
Si Cantare	do hexachord	143, 177
Sing Out	diatonic major	93
Skip to My Lou	do hexachord	129, 151
Suo Gan	do tritonic	96
There's A Hole in the Bucket	do pentatonic	24
Tom Dooley	do pentatonic	54
Tongo	do pentatonic – extended	21, 178
Turn the Glasses Over	do pentatonic – extended	32
Twinkle Little Star	do hexachord	16, 43, 45, 46
Who's That?	do pentatonic	49

Blues Scale Melodies

Song Title	Scale/Mode	Page
Joe Turner Blues	incomplete Blues scale melody	135

La-centered Melodies

Song Title	Scale/Mode	Page
Ah, Poor Bird	implied harmonic minor	64, 172
All the Pretty Little Horses	Æolian	103
Birch Tree, The	la hexachord	73, 173
Chantey	melodic minor	41
Fa La La	Æolian	110
Go Down, Moses	implied harmonic minor	81, 82
If You Dance	la hexachord	89
Jesu, Meine Freude	melodic minor	90, 175
John the Rabbit	la hexachord	57
Joshua Fit the Battle of Jericho	la pentachord	81, 83
My Good Old Man	la pentatonic – extended	25
Skin and Bones	la tetratonic	66
Sweet William	Æolian	18
There Once Was A Man from Calcutta	melodic minor	93
Wade in the Water	implied harmonic minor	99

Modal & Mode-like Melodies

Song Title	Scale/Mode	Page
All the Pretty Little Horses	Æolian	103
Aro Que Nostre Seigne Es Nat	Ionian	152, 173
As I Mee Walkéd	Ionian	126
Fa La La	Æolian	110
God Bless the Moon	sol hexachord	51
Lavender's Blue	Ionian	50
Lo Yisa Goy	sol hexachord	87, 175
Love Learns by Laughing	Ionian w/fi, si, di	112
Maoz Tsur	Ionian melody	153, 176
Non nobis, Domine	Mixolydian	91, 177
O Sacred Head	Phyrgian melody	148, 149
Ol' Gray Goose	Mixolydian	75
Ol' Joe Clark	Mixolydian	69
Sakura	mi pentachord	55, 178
Sweet William	Æolian	18

Time Signatures of ¢, $\frac{2}{4}$, $\frac{4}{4}$, C

Song Title	Time Signature	Page
Ah, Poor Bird	C	64, 172
Ah! Vous Dirai Je, Maman	$\frac{2}{4}$	124, 172
Alouette	$\frac{4}{4}$	138, 172
All the Pretty Little Horses	$\frac{4}{4}$	103
Aunt Rhody	¢	134
Banuwa Yo	$\frac{2}{4}$	86, 173
Birch Tree, The	$\frac{2}{4}$	73, 173
Bobo Leh Me 'Lone	$\frac{4}{4}$	123
Bow Wow Wow	C	62
Buffalo Boy	$\frac{2}{4}$	26
Bye, Bye Baby	$\frac{2}{4}$	101
Catch 'round the Table	C	94
Chantey	$\frac{2}{4}$	41
Dance Josey	$\frac{2}{4}$	30
Devil's Nine Questions, The	¢	60
Do, Re, Mi, Fa	$\frac{4}{4}$	126
Don't Let the Wind	$\frac{4}{4}$	79
Fa La La	$\frac{4}{4}$	110
Go Down, Moses	$\frac{4}{4}$	81, 82
God Bless the Moon	$\frac{4}{4}$	51
Great Big House	$\frac{2}{4}$	63
Hill and Gully Rider	$\frac{4}{4}$	39
Hot Cross Buns	$\frac{4}{4}$	105
Hurry, Hurry, Hurry	$\frac{4}{4}$	80
I Saw the Light	$\frac{4}{4}$	79
If You Dance	$\frac{4}{4}$	89
Jesu, Meine Freude	$\frac{4}{4}$	90, 175
Joe Turner Blues	$\frac{4}{4}$	135
John the Rabbit	$\frac{2}{4}$	57
Johnny On a Woodpile	$\frac{2}{4}$	20
Joshua Fit the Battle of Jericho	$\frac{4}{4}$	81, 83
Lion Sleeps Tonight, The	$\frac{4}{4}$	136
Liza Jane	$\frac{2}{4}$	122
Lo Yisa Goy	$\frac{4}{4}$	87, 175
London Bridge is Falling Down from "Nursery Rhyme Quodlibet"	$\frac{2}{4}$	107
Love Learns by Laughing	C	112
Lucy Locket	$\frac{4}{4}$	105

Song Title	Time Signature	Page
Maoz Tsur	4/4	153, 176
Mary Had A Little Lamb from "Nursery Rhyme Quodlibet"	2/4	107
May Day Carol, The	4/4	102
Mofe Moni S'mo Hogbeke	2/4	85, 176
My Good Old Man	2/4	25
No Need to Hurry	4/4	80
Non nobis, Domine	4/2	91, 177
O Sacred Head	4/4	148, 149
Ol' Gray Goose	2/4	75
Ol' Joe Clark	2/4	69
Ol' Texas	2/4	22
Oleana	2/4	97
Pease Porridge Hot from "Nursery Rhyme Quodlibet"	2/4	107
Rocky Mountain	2/4	67
Sail Away Ladies	2/4	59
Sakura	2/2	55, 178
Sandy Land	2/4	130
Sea Shell	2/4	53
Si Cantare	4/4	143, 177
Sing Out	4/4	93
Skip to My Lou	2/4	129, 151
Snail, Snail	2/4	73
Suo Gan	4/4	96
Sweet William	4/4	18
There Once Was A Man from Calcutta	4/4	93
Tom Dooley	4/4	54
Tongo	2/4	21, 178
Turn the Glasses Over	4/4	32
Twinkle Little Star	2/4	16, 43, 45, 46
Wade in the Water	4/4	99
Who's That?	2/4	49

Time Signatures of $\frac{6}{8}$, $\frac{9}{8}$, $\frac{3}{4}$, $\frac{3}{2}$

Song Title	Time Signature	Page
Aro Que Nostre Seigne Es Nat	$\frac{3}{4}$	152, 173
As I Mee Walkéd	$\frac{4}{2}$	126
Coffee Canon from "Quodlibet in Nine Parts"	$\frac{3}{4}$	109, 176
Come, Let Us All A-Maying Go	$\frac{6}{4}$	40
De Colores	$\frac{6}{8}$	141, 175
Down in the Valley	$\frac{9}{8}$	131
El Flóron	$\frac{6}{8}$	139, 175
Fanny	$\frac{3}{4}$	127
Farmer in the Dell, The	$\frac{6}{8}$	28
Father Grumble	$\frac{6}{8}$	17
Lavender's Blue	$\frac{6}{8}$	50
Let Mirth and Joy A-bound	$\frac{6}{8}$	144
Music Alone Shall Live from "Quodlibet in Nine Parts"	$\frac{3}{4}$	109, 176
Orchestra, The	$\frac{3}{4}$	108, 177
Shepherd, The from "Quodlibet in Nine Parts"	$\frac{3}{4}$	109, 177
Skin and Bones	$\frac{6}{8}$	66
There's A Hole in the Bucket	$\frac{6}{8}$	24

Songs with Complete Texts or Additional Verses in Languages other than English

(see Appendix D, Translation and Adaption of Non-English Text, p. 172)

Song Title	Language	Page
Ah, Poor Bird	German	64, 172
Ah! Vous Dirai Je, Maman	French	124, 172
Alouette	French	138, 172
Aro Que Nostre Seigne Es Nat	Provençal (French)	152, 173
Banuwa Yo	Liberian	86, 173
Birch Tree, The	Russian	73, 173
Coffee Canon from "Quodlibet in Nine Parts"	German	109, 176
De Colores	Spanish	140, 175
El Flóron	Spanish	139, 175
Jesu, Meine Freude	German	90, 175
Lo Yisa Goy	Hebrew	87, 175
Maoz Tsur	Hebrew	153, 176
Mofe Moni S'mo Hogbeke	Yoruban	85, 176
Music Alone Shall Live from "Quodlibet in Nine Parts"	German	109, 176
Non nobis, Domine	Latin	91, 177
Orchestra, The	German	108, 177
Sakura	Japanese	55, 178
Si Cantare	Italian	143, 177
Shepherd, The from "Quodlibet in Nine Parts"	German	109, 177
Tongo	Polynesian	21, 178

Appendix A - Glossary

antiphonal singing – small groups of singers each sing one phrase of a song without stopping between phrases. Referred to as chain phrases when each phrase is sung by an individual rather than a group of singers.

beat – physically keeping the steady pulse to music while stationary, through locomotor movement, or with a body ostinato.

beat division – physically keeping the beat division (whether the beat is divided by 2 or 3 sounds) while singing or listening to music.

call and response – song in which each phrase sung by a group or soloist (call) is answered by another group or soloist with a motif or phrase that is not the same as the call (response). Singing that alternates between a soloist (call) and a congregation (response) in liturgical situations is referred to as responsorial singing.

canon – a melody [subject] sung by one voice part [dux] which is strictly imitated in another voice part [comes]. Voice parts may enter at any interval of duration (canon of one measure, two measures), can be performed in augmentation (twice as slow) or in diminution (twice as fast), and can be sung at the unison or with different intervals between the voices (such as canon at the fifth), and can be performed in inversion, retrograde or retrograde inversion.

canonic singing – songs which are not expressly composed as canons, but can be sung in imitation such as bitonic (sol-mi), tritonic (sol-mi-do), tetratonic (sol-mi-re-do), or pentatonic melodies (la-sol-mi-re-do). Pedagogically referred to as singing in canon.

catch – an English round of the 17th and 18th centuries, canonic in construction. Only when sung in parts would the words from one phrase 'catch' words in another phrase to create a sentence resulting in puns or double entendre.

chain phrases – individual singers sing one phrase of a song in succession without stopping between phrases; also known as relay singing. Referred to as antiphonal singing when phrases are sung by groups of singers rather than individuals.

choral / hymn – Protestant metrical hymn tune originally sung in unison that was then harmonized in multiple-part settings during the 16th-17th centuries. These harmonized melodies are also referred to as hymns.

chord root singing – one group sings the melody of a song while another group sings the chord roots; also referred to as bass line singing or root melody.

comparatives – comparing and identifying things in music that are the same, different, or similar.

counter melody – an independent melody that is subordinate to and often in contrary motion with the melody.

descant – an independent melody that is often higher than and sometimes in contrary motion to the melody.

dialogue song – a song that depicts a conversation between two people.

drone – sustained tone(s), usually lower than the melody. Also referred to as pedal point because on the organ, the drone is generally played on the pedals.

echo song – song in which each phrase sung by a group or soloist is repeated (echoed) exactly by another group or soloist.

glee – an 18th century genre of unaccompanied English choral music in three or more parts for solo men's voices (including male alto); generally brief, constructed in sections, and homophonic. Some glees can be sung by either treble or mixed voices.

hand sign singing – singing in solfège from teacher's hand signs.

harmonic ending – adding a second part (or more) to the final note, notes, or phrase of a song, in order to harmonize a final tonic note as a chord.

homophony – the combination of voice parts of similar rhythmic design with the melody concentrated in one voice part such as melody-plus-accompaniment (singing a song with guitar), or homorhythmic (rhythms are the same or similar among all of the parts) textures found in hymns and chorales.

interval singing – singers sing an interval with solfège and then with the interval name.

layered song – a tune that is comprised of a number of phrases sung repeatedly, one on top of the other.

madrigal – an unaccompanied polyphonic song for two or more voices with secular texts.

ostinati *[plural of ostinato]* – multiple ostinatos performed at the same time.

ostinato, melodic – a motif (short succession of notes) that is repeated at the same pitch throughout a piece of music.

ostinato, rhythmic – a rhythm pattern that is repeated throughout a piece of music.

parallel harmony – adding a line with consistently parallel third intervals or parallel sixth intervals to the melody. Generally, when the melody begins on the tonic or third, the harmony is sung a third above or a sixth below; when the melody begins on the fifth, the harmony is sung a third below or a sixth above.

part-singing – the ability to sing and maintain one's own vocal part in music while another vocal part is being performed simultaneously; includes 2-part (bicinia), 3-part (tricinia), 4-part, and multiple-division vocal music.

part-work – the ability to perform and maintain one's own part in music while another part (instrumental, hand signs, body percussion, rhythmic, melodic, vocal, etc.) is being performed simultaneously; part-singing is a type of part-work.

partner songs – two songs which can be sung simultaneously because they have the same harmonic sequence or the same pentatonic properties. Also called combinable songs.

Appendix A - Glossary, *continued*

polyphony – simultaneous individual voice parts with independent melodic movement.

quodlibet – a collection of two or more tunes, often in no way related, which can be played or sung simultaneously because the progression of harmonic function is the same for each or mixed in some clever way, resulting in great fun or humor for the performer and audience.

rhythm - rhythm is how many sounds are produced on each beat by the text. Rhythm can match the beat, match the beat division, or be different than either the beat or beat division.

rhythm body canon - instead of clapping in a canon, assign each rhythmic element to a specific body part.

rhythm canon - performing a song as the rhythm is clapped in canon.

round – a circular canon with several voices singing the same melody in overlapping succession, all entering on the same pitch as the first voice, returning to the beginning and singing (seemingly) without end. The melody consists of sections of equal length with the same underlying harmonic progression which, when sung together, produce harmony.

singing games – games in which the accompanying music is sung by the participants with the game played by adhering to the text of the song that often includes motions, actions, or competitive rules.

two parts with self – one person simultaneously sings a song while performing a different part through the use of body percussion, rhythm instruments, hand signs, or melodic instruments, etc.

unison singing – simultaneous singing of the same melody at exactly the same pitch.

use of the voice – the voice is produced by a group of muscles that can be exercised, strengthened, and used in many ways such as expressing emotions, dynamics, and articulation.

vocal chording – one group sings the melody while two or more other groups sing the chord tones; chord inversions are often used so that the movement between the tones in each voice part is minimal.

Appendix B - Resources

Barron, J. (1993). *Ride with me: A journey from unison to part-singing (teacher's book).* Ontario, Canada: The Frederick Harris Music Co., Ltd.

Britton, A. P. (1949). Theoretical introductions in American tune-books to 1800 (Doctoral dissertation, University of Michigan, 1949/1950). *Dissertation Abstracts International,* 10/01, ATT 0001505.

Darazs, A., & Jay, S. (1965). *Sight and sound: Visual aid to melody and harmony (teacher's manual)*. New York: Boosey & Hawkes.

Dearborn, K. (1976). But...can Johnny sing? *Keeping Up With Kodály Concepts in Music Education,* 62-65.

Dittemore, E. E. (1970). An investigation of some musical capabilities of elementary school singers (Doctoral dissertation, University of Iowa, 1968/1970). *Dissertation Abstracts International,* 69-8723.

Goetze, M. (1981). Children's singing voices. *Kodály Envoy,* 7 (4), 1-5.

Goetze, M., Broeker, A., & Boshkoff, R. (2009). *Educating young singers: A choral resource for teacher-conductors*. Chicago, IL: GIA Publications, Inc.

Herboly-Kocsár, I. (1984). *Teaching of polyphony, harmony and form in the elementary school.* (A. Farkas, Trans.). Budapest: Péter Erdei.

Houlahan, M., & Tacka, P. (1990). Sound thinking: A suggested sequence for teaching musical elements based on the philosophy of Zoltán Kodály for a college music theory course. *Journal of Music Theory Pedagogy,* 4 (1), 85-109.

Junda, M. E. (1997). Part-singing revisited. *Music Educators Journal,* 83 (6), 35-40.

Kimble, E. P. (1983). The effect of various factors on the ability of children to sing an added part (Doctoral dissertation, University of Georgia, 1983). *Dissertation Abstracts International,* A44/08, ATT 83-26407.

Klinger, R. (1989). Introducing part music to children. *Kodály Envoy,* 15 (4), 21-23.

Lorenz, R. (1995). Canon as a pedagogical tool: Applications from sixteenth-century Wittenberg. *Indiana Theory Review,* 16, 83-104.

McCoy, C. W. (1989). Basic training: Working with inexperienced choirs. *Music Educator's Journal,* 75 (8), 42-45.

Moore, R. S. (1994). Effects of age, sex, and melodic/harmonic patterns on vocal pitch-matching skills of talented 8-11-year-olds. *Journal of Research in Music Education,* 42 (1), 5-13.

Newlin, G. A. (2006). Sequencing part-work for beginning singers. *Choral Journal,* 46 (10), 19-29.

Appendix B - Resources, *continued*

Newlin, G. A. (2004). The Effects of part-work Instruction on first-grade part-singing acquisition and achievement (Doctoral dissertation). *ProQuest Dissertations & Theses Global: The Arts*, 3129412.

Nordholm, H. (1966). *Singing in the elementary schools.* New Jersey: Prentice-Hall, Inc.

Rappaport, J. (1986). The sequential development of part-work. *Kodály Envoy, 12* (3), 4-6.

Swears, L. (1985). *Teaching the elementary school chorus.* West Nyack, NY: Parker Publishing Company, Inc. pp. 118-139.

Vinden, D. (1996). Two at a time. *Music Teacher, 75* (2), 13.

Wolff, C. (2000). *Johann Sebastian Bach: The learned musician.* New York: Norton.

International Phonetic Alphabet
(guide to pronunciation of solfège)

o = [o] as in *gold*

i = [i] as in *green*

a = [a] as in *olive*

e = [e] as in *beige*

sol = [so] *with the "l" silent*

Appendix C - Solfège Syllables

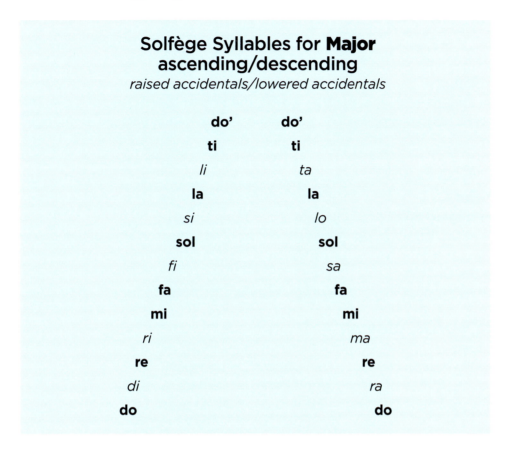

Appendix D
Translation and Adaption of Non-English Text

Transliteration: the characters of each language have been changed into corresponding letters of the English language. In other words, the English words are not translated by meaning of text, only by pronunciation of sounds so sing what you see with English pronunciation.

Ah, Poor Bird
German singing text:
Gute nacht, gute ruh, die Sonne geht schon schlafen, schlafen geh auch du.

English translation:
Good night, good rest, the sun already went to sleep, so as well should you.

Ah! Vous Dirai Je, Maman
French text:
Ah! Vous dirai je, Maman, ce qui cause mon tourment!
Papa veut que je raisonne comme une grande personne;
moi, je dis que les bonbons valent mieux que la raison.

Quand trois poules vont aux champs, La première va devant.
La second' suit la première, La troisiem' vient la dernie're.
Quand trois poules vont aux champs, La première va devant.

English translation:
Ah! Will I tell you, Mommy, what is tormenting me?
Daddy wants me to reason like a grown up person;
Me, I say that sweets are worth more than reason.

When three hens go to the fields, the first goes in front.
The second follows the first, the third comes last.
When three hens go to the fields, the first goes in front.

Alouette
French text:
Alouette, gentille Alouette, Alouette, Je te plumerai.
Et la tête/Et la bec/Et le cou/Et le dos/Et les pattes.

English translation (in retribution for being woken up by the Lark's song):
Lark, nice Lark, Lark, I will pluck you.
I will pluck the head/And the beak/And the neck/And the back/And the legs.

Aro Que Nostre Seigne Es Nat

Provençal (Medieval French) text:

Aro que nostre seigne es nat, Lan drigo driquette lan tiro lira,
Ley menestrié nous van dona cauques oubado,
Beou badau bado, fretillo sautillo, Dre commo faucillo; Fou ben dansa!
Res non bouge sian may de douge, Lan drigo driquette lan tiro lira.

English translation:

Now that our Lord is Born,
The minstrels are going to give us some serenades.
Wriggle, jump about, straight as a sickle, let's dance!
Do not move, we are more than twice twelve.

Banuwa Yo

Liberian text:

Banuwa, banuwa, banuwa yo.
A la no nehnia la no.

English translation:

Don't cry, little girl.

English singing adaption:

Sing noel, sing noel, sing we noel.
Sing we all noel.

The Birch Tree

Russian TRANSLITERATED text:

Vo polye byeryoza stayala,
Vo polye kudryavaya stayala.
Lyuli, lyuli, stayala.
Lyuli, lyuli, stayala.

Nyekomu byeryozu zalomati,
Nyekomu kudryavu zashtshipati,
Lyuli, lyuli, zalomati.
Lyuli, lyuli, zalomati.

Paidu ya v lyes, pagulyayu,
Byeluyu byeryozu zalomayu,
Lyuli, lyuli, pagulyayu,
Lyuli, lyuli, zalomayu.

Appendix D, *continued*

The Birch Tree, continued

    Srezhu ya z byeryozyy tri prutotshka,
    Zdyelayu iz nyikh ya tri gudotshka,
    Lyuli, lyuli, tri prototshka,
    Lyuli, lyuli, tri gudotshka.

    Tshetvertuya balalaiku,
    Staromu dyedu na zabavku,
    Lyuli, lyuli, balalaiku,
    Lyuli, lyuli, na zabavku.

English singing adaption (not a direct translation):
    See the lovely birch in the meadow,
    Curly leaves are dancing when the wind blows.
    Liuli, liuli the wind blows.
    Liuli, liuli in the meadow.

    No one here would hurt you, O birch tree.
    Where is he who does not love the birch tree?
    Liuli, liuli O birch tree.
    Liuli, liuli O birch tree.

    I will go alone to the forest,
    I will cut the birch in the forest,
    Liuli, liuli, the forest,
    Liuli, liuli, the forest.

    O my little tree, I need three branches;
    For three silver pipes, I need three branches.
    Liuli, liuli, three branches,
    Liuli, liuli, three branches.

    When I play my new balalaika,
    I will sing of you, my little birch tree.
    Liuli, liu, I'll be playing
    Liuli, liu, little birch tree.

De Colores

Spanish text:
De colores, de colores se visten los campos en la primavera.
De colores, de colores son los pajaritos que vienen deafuera.
De colores, de colores es el arco iris que vemos lucir.
Y por eso los grandes amores de muchos colores me gustan a mí.
Y por eso los grandes amores de muchos colores me gustan a mí.

English translation:
In colors, in colors the fields are dressed in the spring.
In colors, in colors are the little birds that fly outside.
In colors, in colors is the rainbow that we see shining.
And that is why I love the great loves of many colors.
And that is why I love the great loves of many colors.

El Flóron

Spanish text:
El florón pasó por aqui, Yo no lo vi, yo no lo vi.
Que pase, que pase, que pase el florón.

English translation:
A flower passed through here, I didn't see it, I didn't see it.
Passing, passing, passing the flower.

Jesu, Meine Freude

German text:
Jesu, meine Freude, meines Herzens Weide, Jesu, meine Zier;
Ach, wie lang, ach lange ist dem Herzen bange und verlangt nach dir!
Gottes Lamm, mein Braütigam, ausser dir soll mir auf Erden nichts sonst Liebers werden.

English translation:
Jesus, my joy, my heart's delight, Jesus, my treasure,
How long, ah, how long my heart is anxious and longs for you!
God's lamb, my bridegroom, nothing on earth is dearer to me than you.

Lo Yisa Goy

Hebrew text:
Lo yisa goy goy el goy cherev, v'lo yil me du od milchama.

English translation:
Nation shall not lift up sword against nation, nor ever again shall they rise for war.

Appendix D, *continued*

Maoz Tsur
Hebrew text:
Maoz tsur y'shuati, l'cha naeh l'shabeach.
Tikon bet t'filati v'sham toda n'zabeach.
L'et tachin matbeach, mitsar hamnabeach;
Az egmor b'shir mizmor hanukat hamizbeach.

English translation:
Rock of ages, let our song, praise thy saving power.
Thou, amidst the raging foes, was our sheltering tower.
Furious they assailed us, but thine arm availed us,
And thy word broke their sword, when our own strength failed us.

Mofe Moni S'mo Hogbeke
Yoruban text:
Mofe Moni S'mo Hogbeke.

English singing adaption (not a translation):
Everybody loves Saturday night.

"Quodlibet in Nine Parts"
Coffee Canon
German text:
C-A-F-F-E-E, trink nicht so viel Caffee,
Nicht für kinder ist der Türken trank, schwächt die Nerven, macht die blass und Krank.
Sei doch kein Muselmann, der ihn nicht lassen kann.

English translation:
C-O-F-F-E-E, don't drink so much coffee,
Not for children is this Turkish drink, it makes you nervous, pale and sick.
Don't be like the muscle man who can't give it up.

Music Alone Shall Live
German text:
Himmel und erde Mussen vergehn.
Aber die Musica, Aber die Musica,
Aber die Musica, Bleiben bestehn.

English translation:
Heaven and earth must pass away,
But the music, but the music,
But the music remains enduring.

Shepherd, The
German text:
Es tönen die Lieder Der Frühling kehrt wieder
Es spieled der Hirte Auf seiner Schalmei:
La-la-la-la-la-la-la-la-la-la, La-la-la-la-la-la-la!

English translation:
It tones the songs of spring's return
Thus played the shepherd on his shawm:
La-la-la-la-la-la-la-la-la-la, La-la-la-la-la-la-la!

Si Cantare
Italian text:
Si cantare (la la la), cosi l'ore ne passara.

English translation:
We sing (la la la), so it will pass the hours.

Non nobis, Domine
Latin text:
Non nobis, Domine, sed nomini tuo da gloriam.

English translation:
Not unto us, O Lord, but unto thy name is all glory given.

The Orchestra
German text:
- (Violin) Die Geige, sie singt, sie jubelt und klingt. (2x)
- (Clarinet) Die Klarinett, die Klarinett, macht duaduadua gar so nett. (2x)
- (Trumpet) Die Trompete, die schmettert: tätätätäteterätätätätäteterä
  Die Trompete, die schmettert: tätätätäteterätätätätä.
- (Horn) Das Horn, das Horn, das ruht sich aus. (2x)
- (Drum) Die Paule hat's leicht den sie spielt nur zwei Töne:
  Fünf – eins, eins – fünf, bum bum bum bum bum.

English translation:
- (Violin) The violin, she sings, she cheers and sounds.
- (Clarinet) The clarinet does not sound so nice going doodle-det.
- (Trumpet) The trumpet blares ta-ta-ta.
- (Horn) The horns rest themselves (on this one note).
- (Drum) The drum has it so easy, it only plays two tones:
  Five – one, one – five, five, five, five, five, one.

Appendix D, *continued*

Sakura

Japanese TRANSLITERATED text:
Sakura, sakura
Yayoi no sorawa,
Miwatasu kagiri.
Kasumi ka kumoka?
Nioi zo izuru.
Iza ya, iza ya
Mi ni yukaun.

English translation:
Cherry blossoms, cherry blossoms,
Across the spring sky,
As far as the eye can see.
Is it fog or is it a cloud?
Fragrant scent in the air.
Right now, right now,
Let's go and see them.

Tongo

Polynesian TRANSLITERATED text:
Tongo;
Jimnee bye bye oh;
Oom bah deh kim bye oh;
Ooh ah-ay;
Mahleh ka-ah lo way.

English description:
This song depicts people communicating across the water as they paddle past each other in long boats.

Index of Topics and Song Titles

Topics and Song Titles	Page
Ah, Poor Bird	64, 172
Ah! Vous Dirai Je, Maman	124, 172
Alouette	138, 172
All the Pretty Little Horses	103
antiphonal singing	47
Aro Que Nostre Seigne Es Nat	152, 173
As I Mee Walkéd	126
Aunt Rhody	134
Banuwa Yo	86, 173
beat	34
beat division	35
Birch Tree, The	73, 173
Bobo Leh Me 'Lone	123
Bow Wow Wow	62
Buffalo Boy	26
Bye, Bye Baby	101
call and response	56
canon	88
canonic singing	72
catch	92
Catch 'round the Table	94
chain phrases	52
Chantey	41
chorale / hymn	147
chord root singing	127
Coffee Canon from "Quodlibet in Nine Parts"	109, 176
Come, Let Us All A-Maying Go	40
comparatives	12
counter melody	100
Dance Josey	30
De Colores	140, 175
descant	95
Devil's Nine Questions, The	60
dialogue song	23
Do, Re, Mi, Fa	126
Don't Let the Wind	79
Down in the Valley	131
drone	61
echo song	19
El Flóron	139, 175
Fa La La	110

Topics and Song Titles	Page
Fanny	127
Farmer in the Dell, The	28
Father Grumble	17
glee	**142**
Go Down, Moses	81, 82
God Bless the Moon	51
Great Big House	63
hand sign singing	**117**
harmonic ending	**120**
Hill and Gully Rider	39
homophony	**150**
Hot Cross Buns	105
Hurry, Hurry, Hurry	80
I Saw the Light	79
If You Dance	89
interval singing	**119**
Jesu, Meine Freude	90, 175
Joe Turner Blues	135
John the Rabbit	57
Johnny On a Woodpile	20
Joshua Fit the Battle of Jericho	81, 83
Lavender's Blue	50
layered song	**84**
Let Mirth and Joy A-bound	144
Lion Sleeps Tonight, The	136
Liza Jane	122
Lo Yisa Goy	87, 175
London Bridge is Falling Down from "Nursery Rhyme Quodlibet"	107
Love Learns by Laughing	112
Lucy Locket	105
madrigal	**110**
Maoz Tsur	153, 176
Mary Had A Little Lamb from "Nursery Rhyme Quodlibet"	107
May Day Carol, The	102
melodic ostinato	**65**
Mofe Moni S'mo Hogbeke	85, 176
Music Alone Shall Live from "Quodlibet in Nine Parts"	109, 176
My Good Old Man	25
No Need to Hurry	80
Non nobis, Domine	91, 177
O Sacred Head	148, 149
Ol' Gray Goose	75

Topics and Song Titles	Page
Ol' Joe Clark	69
Ol' Texas	22
Oleana	97
Orchestra, The	108, 177
ostinati	**42, 66**
parallel harmony	137
part-singing	8
part-work	8
partner songs	77
Pease Porridge Hot from "Nursery Rhyme Quodlibet"	107
polyphony	115
quodlibet	106
rhythm	36
rhythm body canon	44
rhythm canon	44
rhythmic ostinato	37
Rocky Mountain	67
round	125
Sail Away Ladies	59
Sakura	55, 178
Sandy Land	130
Scales	118
Sea Shell	53
Shepherd, The from "Quodlibet in Nine Parts"	109, 177
Si Cantare	143, 177
Sing Out	93
singing games	27
Skin and Bones	66
Skip to My Lou	129, 151
Snail, Snail	73
Suo Gan	96
Sweet William	18
There Once Was A Man from Calcutta	93
There's A Hole in the Bucket	24
Tom Dooley	54
Tongo	21, 178
Turn the Glasses Over	32
Twinkle Little Star	16, 43, 45, 46
two parts with self in homophony	141
two parts with self in polyphony	104
unison singing	15
use of the voice	14
vocal chording	132
Wade in the Water	99
Who's That?	49

About the Author

Georgia A. Newlin

Georgia A. Newlin, DMA is Associate Professor of Music Education at Adelphi University on Long Island, NY. She taught in early childhood and public school music positions for fifteen years.

Currently, Dr. Newlin is called upon as a conductor for elementary, middle and high school choral festivals. She is a master teacher at the Summer Kodály Institute at Indiana University, University of Hawai'i Kodály Levels, and the Kodály Institute at James Madison University.

Georgia is Past President of the Organization of American Kodály Educators and is a member of The VoiceCare Network. She has been a presenter for numerous music associations and conferences at local, state, national and international levels. She has had articles and choral octavo reviews published in journals such as the *Choral Journal, Orff Echo, Kodály Envoy,* and *Southwestern Musician*. Her arrangement of "Es ist ein' Ros' 'entsprungen" is available from Colla Voce as part of the *Ruth Dwyer Choral Series*. In addition, she has joined the team of the *Crooked River Choral Project* creating lesson plans for teaching music literacy through choral singing available from Music Is Elementary.

Georgia holds a Doctor of Musical Arts in Pedagogy from the Hartt School at the University of Hartford, a Master of Music in Music Education with Kodály Emphasis from Holy Names College, and a Bachelor of Science in Music Education from West Chester University.

Dr. Newlin considers herself most fortunate in that she has been able to spend her life making music with others and has actually been paid for it.